Witnesses

Witnesses

Clark Sturges

Diablo Valley College

The Glendessary Press, Inc. — Berkeley

Printed in the United States of America
Published by the Glendessary Press, Inc.
ISBN # 0-87709-221-4
LC No.: 73-88640

ACKNOWLEDGMENTS

I would like to thank these advisors for their help in preparing and reviewing *Witnesses:* C. H. Gustafson, Roberta Hussey, Wendell Johnson, Robert Martincich, Marilyn Shoemaker, William Sparke (all of Diablo Valley College), Nicholas Furtado, Richard Kuhn, and my wife, Barbara. In addition, I appreciate the contributions of Joan Herschel Parsons, president of The Glendessary Press; and Bill Rock, typesetter.

For Lindsay and Jeffrey

CONTRIBUTORS

Edmund V. Aversenti, Jr. — p. 83
Susan Carey — p. 25
Jennie R. Cavallaro — p. 17
Nancy Charles — pp. 68, 115
Deborah Day — p. 49
Don C. DeWitt — p. 74
Janet Lynn Ferman — p. 111
Stephen Gerber — p. 93
Pat Haas — p. 128
Donna Hagerstrand — p. 52
Debbie Henderson — p. 87
Ken Henry
Robin Ann Johnson — p. 28
Kristine Kesler — p. 71
Robert W. Krull

Sherri Lindahl
Ms. Nancy Long
Jim McBride
Dale Miller
Valerie Okrongly — p. 57
Joseph J. Pribela — p. 136
Carol Rogers
Marjorie Rolandelli
Peggy Ross — p. 102
Harvey W. Roth — p. 60
Joelyn Ryan — pp. 33, 125
John Simmen — p. 43
Shirley Smith — pp. 55, 65
Sydney Stephens
Ronald R. Vanderbout — pp. 40, 99

(Several writers chose to exclude page references.)

PREFACE

Witnesses is a collection of papers written by college students enrolled in required freshman composition classes. They were asked to emphasize their own experience in their writing. Few of the students plan to major in English, and few began their study by admitting that they liked to write or that they thought writing was easy. What value does this collection have, a book written by amateurs, nonwriters? And why personal experience writing?

In my classes I want my students to understand, first of all, that writing is more than the transfer of ideas from one person to another. It is also a process that helps to create and define the writer's perceptions and character. In other words, the writer discovers some of what he has to say, and thus some of himself, as he writes, not before he writes. And second, I want my students to leave my classes convinced that they have the ability to write clearly and effectively without undue hesitation, apprehension, or frustration. Not surprisingly, their best writing comes from what they know well—the people and events that make up their own lives.

When I say that writing is a process of discovery, I'm not suggesting that the discovery is necessarily dramatic. When a writer begins to focus and shape his knowledge of a friend or event, he becomes aware of nuances, shadings, sensitivities, and blind spots. This developing awareness can gradually give the writer a new perspective.

There are, of course, a number of textbooks that include personal experience writing, but they almost all feature professional writers. A major advantage of *Witnesses,* I believe, is its emphasis on writing by nonprofessionals, by students much like those who will read and study the book. Since the writing in *Witnesses* reflects confidence, readers should feel encouraged about their own abilities to write effectively. For the most part the writers of *Witnesses* control well what they have to say — they have a clear purpose and they accomplish it.

Later on I'll illustrate some specific approaches for analyzing one of the papers, but first there are a few general comments I want to make about this book. *Witnesses* is a starting point. While it will be fruitful for students to read and discuss this collection, I think too they should add to it. A good class project would be a supplement or addendum to *Witnesses,* perhaps a magazine printed on ditto or a binder of original work that could be checked out or passed around.

Can this book tie into journal writing? Journal entries are often probes, beginnings, or rambling explorations which frequently can be sources for more carefully and completely shaped pieces of writing. I can see a journal as the first stage in a two-stage program of personal experience writing. *Witnesses* reflects this possibility clearly in the number of papers that rely on observation and description.

Witnesses avoids the traditional textbook apparatus of discussion questions, applications, and suggestions for further study, because I believe the book can be used most profitably when the instructor creates his or her own critical and analytical methods. To test this belief I asked several of my colleagues to use the first paper in the book in at least one of their composition classes. I gave few instructions, other than to say I wanted a brief report of what they had done and the chance to look through any student writing that resulted from their experiments. Here are some of their approaches along with brief excerpts from student responses.

I began by explaining that every writer leaves his thumbprint on his work. Then I asked the students to write a profile sketch of the author of this essay on the basis of what was written.

"I can't get over the thoughts she has written down and how they resemble my own thoughts of a boy I've known for years. Both she and I have a maternal attitude and we show it in similar ways. The idea of looking after someone and being needed and appreciated is very important to both of us."

First we discussed the paper. Then I asked for in-class writing that "should touch" the example in some way, perhaps as an imitation of it or as a continuation.

"This paper shouldn't be difficult to write. I have known her for some time now. The changes in her physically have been few. Mentally, the changes have been numerous. Don't get me wrong. I'm not analytical. I don't attach labels, especially on a friend who treats me good. She is perceptive about changes and the only irony of the situation is she can't tell the changes that have taken place in herself."

"There she sits, the stranger. I don't even know her name, but somehow I feel I know her. She's warm and friendly looking, but I imagine she's shy and quiet. But there is something deeper hiding behind the outer appearance. If you look deep into her eyes, you may be able to glimpse it. I saw it once, but she quickly turned away to keep me from seeing it clearly."

Read the student paper. Write a description of someone you know well. Reread the handout and discuss how that piece compares to yours.

"Comparing this description with the one of the person I wrote about brings out two different ways of describing people. In this paper, the writer emphasized the physical aspects. She described how she felt about him when they first met and how she feels about him now — even though she doesn't know a lot about him or hasn't found out everything there is to know about him. She describes his physical features with some detail — spending separate paragraphs on his eyes, nose, mouth and teeth, hair, and clothes. The writer gives a small hint of his personality, but is mainly interested in his appearance.

"The paper that I wrote describing a friend used another way of describing people. I concentrated on giving a background of the person with details about his life and how he lived. I didn't write about his physical appearance because I think to really describe a person you should write about his background, family, personality, and other things. Physical appearance is secondary in describing what a person is really like."

Read the student paper. Choose someone in this class who is in some way like the writer of this paper. Explain.

"The one in our class that makes me think of the author is small, has short, shaggy blond hair, and nervous eyes. She looks like she might want to be a model. She has a cute pixie face and I hate her for her shape, but I wouldn't want her personality. She dresses well and looks like the type that would think that someone who was 17 was 'foxy.' As for full lips being sensuous, well, different strokes for different folks, as the saying goes."

Read the student paper and choose a photograph from your text that connects; explain.

[A photograph of a woman flying a kite.] "The reason I picked this picture is because I found various sentences in the writing that clued me as to what kind of a person the writer is. The main sentence that sticks out in my mind is the one where she says, 'I'm impulsive and emotive.' In the picture the woman is very expressive with her body in getting the kite to fly. Her emotions seem to come freely and easily."

[A photograph of two people, probably dancers, facing each other, with a large shadow behind one of them.] "I suppose the picture shown here illustrates the way I see most people. Both youths are staring at one another in silence. They see each other's physical characteristics, but they don't see what makes each one of them a distinct individual, that which I like to think of as being represented by the shadow on the wall."

* * *

I hope these examples are helpful in showing how to use one paper. Each group of papers in *Witnesses* is different, and teaching approaches will vary according to the nature of the papers.

The instructor who asked his class to relate a piece of writing to a photograph might have chosen a picture from *Witnesses.* The photographs I've included show people, scenes, and situations that should stimulate writing. The large photographs, too, divide the book into eight sections or groups and serve as bridges between these classifications. Though none of the photographs are meant to illustrate particular papers, there are both obvious and subtle relationships between the visual images and the text.

Likewise, there are threads that unify the eight groups of papers. The sections aren't labeled, and the threads I see aren't traditional rhetorical or thematic ones, e.g., Description, Comparison and Contrast, Alienation. What's important are the relationships readers see, and students may want to reclassify some parts, creating groups that make more sense to them.

Are the papers in *Witnesses* edited? Most are printed without change. For some, however, I did correct misspellings and make slight revisions in phrasing. I recognize the argument that student writing should be presented exactly as it's written, but I decided to make the changes I described because I thought they were the ones the writers would have made, had the publishing process allowed for more consultation and revision. When the writers gave me permission to use their work, they included permission for minor changes.

A principal intent of this book is to change attitudes about writing and to renew interest in writing as process. The success of this book, of course, depends on what happens to the writing of those who read it. I hope *Witnesses* helps to promote learning and discovery for both students and teachers.

C. S.
Walnut Creek
California

*T*his paper is going to be difficult to write. I have been sitting here for 10 minutes now, sifting through ideas and approaches, staring out my window at masses of green leaves — a voice asks if 7 times 8 is 56. "Yes," I answer. It's a man's voice — but not really a man's and not exactly a boy's voice. The voice belongs to a person with whom I have spent nearly two years. Eating and laughing together, working, learning, and occasionally spending a night together.

I remember when I first saw him and thought how young, skinny, and foxy he was. Now, at 19, he's still skinny, but his shoulders have broadened and the lines of his jaw have become more angular, more masculine, yet at the same time there is something terribly young and even feminine about his face — no, I can't really pinpoint it. Perhaps it's his hair, blond and not quite shoulder length. He always parts it in the middle and it falls in curls and waves, kind of fluffy around his face, which makes his face look narrower than it is. It's cut away shorter at his forehead, almost like bangs, and gradually tapers to its full length along the sides of his face. I know because I'm the one who cuts it.

Small, mutable eyes that can't decide if they're blue or green are protected by brown, perfectly curled eyelashes. The eyebrows are thick, but not bushy, dark blond and gently curved.

17

His nose unmistakably resembles his mom's—not too long or wide and slightly turned up and rounded at the tip. Sort of an ordinary, everyday one, as far as noses go, except that the tip of his nose is almost imperceptibly bent to the left. You have to know about it before you can really see it.

His lips are very full and sensuous and always pink. Behind his lips is a set of straight, widely spaced teeth—the widest space being between his two front teeth. I can't remember if he ever showed me, but I'd bet that he could shoot a nice stream of water through his front teeth. I think he only has about four cavities to his name, but his teeth are dingy because he smokes too much and drinks gallons of strong tea. When he smiles tiny dimples surround his mouth, but just say a word about it and he denies their existence vehemently.

The clothes he wears—better yet his uniform—consist of a long-sleeve khaki shirt (which he varies every once in a great while with a red long-sleeve tailored shirt or a blue work shirt), blue flared Levi jeans, square-toed boots, and a brown leather belt that he bought in front of Cody's in Berkeley for $8. He never buttons his shirt all the way up nor does he ever button the cuffs. Usually his socks are mismatched or, if he has the good fortune to pick two of the same color, one is most likely inside out. However, the inability to choose socks properly is by no means indicative of his mental capacity. His intellect is above average. He is part thinker and part logician and it frustrates me because I'm impulsive and emotive.

Last semester he read a tremendous amount of material, mostly on philosophers, since philosophy is his main interest now; occasionally, though, he threw in some Dostoevski and *Playboy*—if one actually reads *Playboy*. God knows he'd probably read until his eyes fell out, if he could. His hero is Goethe's Mephistopheles, because of his wit and coolness.

I think he's about the biggest bullshitter around and he can have me believing almost anything, but I'm exceptionally gullible to begin with (which I like to say is because of a sincere trust in mankind and

18

not because of naiveté on my part). At times he is critical and skepti-
cal, but I know he's more sensitive than he'll ever let show on the
surface.

While I know a lot about him now, I'll have to wait until later to
say more. There's still much for me to find out.

*H*e was indeed strange. His entire life with us was strange. He was a very vague man, especially in his teaching. It would not have surprised me to discover him completely forgetting about school from the final afternoon bell until morning roll. He never once fit into the mold of a high school psychology teacher, but for being one he drew his monthly check.

Without much effort I can recall a time when, staring out across the sparse campus lawn, I caught sight of his form lying spread-eagle in the noonday sun. My shoulders hunched, and hands buried deep in corduroy pockets, I sauntered over to where he lay. He fit in so well with that ragged lawn, hardly the man one would have expected to be a teacher. He rivalled any of us in dress and appearance—a style that offended our parents' notion of proper grooming. Curled hair that was too long to be down over his ears. Clothes that looked as if slept in: a striped green pull-over shirt, faded pants, and worn tennis shoes whose strings had been several times pitifully repaired in small knots.

Lying there, his hands were in motion. Both left and right, all 10 fingers moving in a pattern; thumb lightly touching forefinger, then index, ring, small, back to ring, index, and forefinger. Back down again finger by finger, back and forth, one by one, slowly, rhythmically, the only sign of life from his sprawled form.

My shadow crossed his resting eyelids, and they opened. His

fingers abruptly ceased their movement. He sat up. He squinted painfully in the light, drawing together the swollen bags beneath his eyes that told of the many wakeful hours he spent the previous evening. There were times when he would tell us on a Monday morning how he had spent the weekend in the snow-covered Sierras backpacking and hiking, with little more than six hours sleep total for the entire trip. There were those of us who didn't believe him. But before the semester was out, I knew better than to doubt.

On went the prescription sunglasses with the cracked lens that was never repaired. In the sunlight we never saw his eyes. In the dimmed classroom we saw bleary, tired eyes.

In the beginning I asked: What's wrong with this guy? I was the only one to have ever stopped asking. He lived in Concord with his wife and two children, but the telephone number he always gave to interested students was in Berkeley, where he lived at times with several others, most of them younger than himself. He was 35, but before I knew I had guessed 10 years younger.

As I said, he taught psychology. "Psychology is the study of one's self." I wasn't very pleased with his definition. Psychology had been my fondest interest for the past years. I had read Perls, Rogers, Jung, textbooks, reprints, and magazines. His statement seemed to be as shoddy as his appearance.

Diagrams flashed on the chalkboard along with a constant flow of explanations. "Man is a process of innumerable 'I's that are constantly changing, each demanding to be called the true self." Two points on the chalkboard, and a line starting from one, but never reaching the other, bending at some mysteriously calculated angle, "We begin with an aim or a goal, but we never reach it. We are subject to 'laws' that often leave us finding ourselves exactly at that point from which we began."

We could never find out from where he drew his ideas. He was always hurried, darting from this to that, without form or direction. "Go toward that which is difficult," he told me once, when his eyes were visibly blurred from lack of sleep. "Make efforts."

What sort of efforts did he expect?

We were lined up standing in rows, the desks pushed back against the walls, doors locked, drapes pulled and the lights dimmed. There we stood, safe from unwelcome eyes in our very unusual psychology class.

He led; 30 responded. Right foot forward, back. Left foot forward, back. Right foot to the right, back. Left foot to the left, back. A step behind, left and right. Then repeat. Right, left, right, left, right left; one, two, three, four, one, two, three, four, one, two, three, four . . .

Up went the right arm, then down, keeping time with the meter of our steps. Left arm up, then back again. Right arm out to the side, then down. Left arm out to the other side, down again.

Now the heads of 30 seniors turned to the right, following 30 extended right arms. Then to the left, then up, then down, and always to the rhythm of our calculated steps. One, two, three, four . . . one, two, three, four.

I remember watching him as best I could through these exercises, waiting for a mistimed move, a wrong direction. But these never came. He moved with an exacting precision.

The class, on the other hand, fared quite miserably, our concentration and sadly underdeveloped coordination hardly adequate for the task. Embarrassed chatter, uneasy giggles:

"Let's remain quiet and concentrate on the positions." We fumbled out of step.

"Let's begin again." Our positions were in poor posture.

"Each position is quite definite. Keep to it." Our meter fumbled again.

"Concentrate." Why?

Always the unasked question of why. But we continued; for them, it was obligation. For me, I wanted to uncover those secrets.

More exercises. We sat in a circle, legs crossed, counting out a rhythm with our hands striking our knees. Two hands for two knees, then left hand on floor, continuing the rhythm, then right hand, then both. Hands into the air, then to sides, then repeat, never altering the precise timing and meter.

"Breathe deeply and slowly, into the diaphragm. Relax, don't strike hard."

Why?

In our conversations, a certain amount of probing began to reveal the information I sought, the information he had been keeping from us so well. He gave me names and titles, but never casually. Often he would caution me to secrecy, even once quickly demanding silence when I mentioned an author's name in class.

Names, titles. They came from an almost unknown tradition in the East. The names were hard for my Western tongue to pronounce, and the titles were as puzzling as the texts, and always almost impossible to locate in bookstores.

Then, quite strangely, he started to refer to me as his teaching assistant. According to him I had done some outside work at the University, which wasn't true. He had me explain certain concepts to the class — those new ideas about which I had just begun reading.

I watched as he interacted with the others. What I once took to be his harmless eccentricities now revealed themselves to be various roles within a complex game he played with us. His students became enchanted, outraged, possessed, humiliated.

With the others he gained a reputation as a benevolent, concerned counselor, ready and willing to give advice and just listen. I came to be avoided. He began to throw every possible obstacle in my way, and answered what few questions he did with hazy, half-truth explanations: "Psychology as a discipline applies only to men, not to machines. We must make the effort to transform ourselves from machines to men."

He took me and two of my close friends to the house in Berkeley. Before the evening was finished, we were dripping in sweat, trying to follow the intensely complicated exercises he gave us. The demand on the body was almost nothing in comparison with the mental and emotional demands. But at the end of each session, I felt invigorated with an unfamiliar yet vital strength.

Then things began to plummet down hill. The amount of attention he gave his second-semester classes was at best a series of token efforts. His lectures decreased and his planning became all but negligent. His memory became dull. On a weekend trip he lost a large set of keys, which meant he was unable to drive back to open his own house or the classroom doors.

Conflicts with the school administration increased. Heated arguments ensued. He confided in me that he most likely would be fired at the end of the semester.

On it went this way for several months. I knew nothing of what was going on in his private life, but I guessed that this was a time of upheaval. Yet through all this his teaching to me increased. I began to glimpse a greater realm with more fantastic implications and possibilities than had ever before been granted. Finally, on a day when I was torn between frustration and commitment, when the immensity of the demands were weighed against the value of the possible attainments, I approached him and asked forthright to enter into a serious study of the ideas he had let me glimpse. He agreed, acting like my request had been predestined from the beginning.

Four days later without drama or fanfare, his car slid out of control on a slippery street, shearing off a power pole. This final collision took from the world forever him and his secrets.

*J*udd was a bad boy, a brat, a behavior problem, a menace. He was only five years old, but adults trembled at his approach. You never knew what he would do next. He might scream at you or call you names, or he might throw a rock at you or kick you in the shins. Or he might just throw some dishes on the floor or break another child's toy.

Judd's misbehavior was a favorite topic of conversation among the members of our church, so it was with some dismay that I learned that he would be in the kindergarten Sunday school class that I had volunteered to teach. Then one day I overheard someone say, "They're making a big mistake, assigning Sue to teach kindergarten. None of us can handle Judd, and we're adults with children of our own. She's only 17 — she'll never be able to do it."

I was not discouraged or frightened by those words; I took them as a challenge. I would prove that a teenager could succeed where all the adults had failed. But how? I was aware that there was something called "child psychology" which was followed religiously by most of the parents I knew. I considered studying it but came to the conclusion that I would be wasting my time. It obviously didn't work. Our congregation included a pediatrician and a psychiatrist, both of whom must have been experts in child psychology, but they got attacked as frequently as anyone else. No, it was obvious that books wouldn't help me. I would have to figure out something on my own.

I began to observe the way the adults treated Judd to find out what they were doing wrong. I saw that the reaction of almost every adult to Judd's approach was, "Oh, no, here comes Judd. What's he going to do this time? I wish he'd get out of here and quit bothering me." Could it be, I wondered, that since Judd was always expected to misbehave he was just doing what he knew was expected of him? I began to feel sorry for Judd. How terribly sad, I thought, to be told constantly, even if not in words, "I don't like you and I don't want you around."

So as I developed my plan for dealing with Judd I was also developing compassion for him. No one but me seemed to realize that there might be some good in Judd. I would show Judd that I loved him and enjoyed having him around. I would make it clear that I expected not just obedience but responsibility and cooperation, and I would let him know that I expected our time together to be enjoyable.

When Judd arrived on the first day of Sunday school I greeted him warmly, which seemed to surprise and please him. But when I told the class that I was going to read a story Judd announced defiantly, "I don't want to hear a story. I want to play with blocks." "All right," I said, "but play quietly so everyone else can hear." He spent the whole first class playing by himself. Once he started throwing blocks, but I just told him firmly, but gently, that throwing things wasn't allowed in Sunday school. That was the last "problem" I had with Judd.

When he came in the second week he headed straight for the blocks. I didn't say anything then, but later, as we were about to begin a new activity, I said, "Judd, we'd like you to play with us. It's going to be fun, and we don't want you to miss it." He joined in joyfully, and from then on he participated in every class. Soon he was

26

helping me serve refreshments, enormously proud that he could pour the juice without spilling a drop.

On the Sunday before Christmas there was to be a special family service, including a candle-lighting ceremony. Each teacher was to select two children from her class to light candles. Judd was my first choice. There was a lot of head-shaking about my decision. "He'll ruin the whole ceremony," they told me. "Why don't you pick someone else?" But my confidence in Judd prevailed, and he was allowed to take part in the ceremony.

When Judd's turn came I could sense the whole congregation holding its breath. (Would he knock down all the lighted candles or set another child on fire?) Judd must have sensed it too, because he turned to look at me, momentarily doubtful. I gave him a smile of reassurance and then watched with tears in my eyes as he proudly moved forward and lit his candle.

I remember him most when it rains. We'd wait until his parents went to bed, then sneak out to the little trailer in the back yard. A mad dash across the wet grass, then into the cold darkness of the trailer. We had a nest there — a pile of sleeping bags in the lower bunk. With the upper bunk close above us, it was like a cave. He would light a candle while I stood shivering, then we would make love in the flickering dimness. We'd hold each other close against the chill and drift with the tinny rattle of the rain on the roof.

Our days seemed to melt into one another, passing quietly as dry leaves falling into a still pond. Two years disappeared as softly as a sigh.

Like old people we took refuge in ourselves, seeking not the excitement sought so desperately by our peers. We went to the library at least once a week, to movies occasionally, and sometimes to the beach. We closed ourselves in, lying together with our books, sharing quiet fantasies.

Ours was, in many ways, a mute relationship. Our words barely scratched the surface. Neither of us worked enough to open the door between us. We had trapped ourselves like pieces on a chessboard. We played the game, neither of us strong enough to break the pattern. Rather than talk problems out, we retreated into hurt silence. Resentments built, resulting in hidden bitterness. Sometimes we found it hard even to say simply, "I love you."

But we were in love. However immature, we loved each other and we tried to pretend that we were "forever." We held on to our security although we both knew that we would eventually separate.

I met him during my third year in high school. A tall, broad guy, he walked upright — never slouched, almost to the point of stiffness. Though straight-bridged, his nose was large above a small firm-lipped mouth. His eyebrows, while not bushy, grew to a point in the middle of the bridge of his nose, giving him a rather fierce expression at times. His almost square, large-framed glasses gave him a general attitude of seriousness and dignity.

He was intelligent — a word-master. He had insight — he could find a person's weaknesses and win almost any sparring match easily with his probing stiletto tongue. He was cynical — sometimes bitter. A disillusioned idealist at age 17. There were a great many people who disliked him, perhaps some who even hated him. He had few close friends.

But he could be charming at times. With his mastery of words, he found flattery an easy game.

I, like most people, disliked him at first, went to great lengths to avoid him. He waited for me after school, as we both walked in the same direction. I tried various tactics to deter him, being at times exceedingly unpleasant. Yet still he persisted, never pushy, just always there. Finally, it was as if all my resistances were worn down — as if he had crashed through a barrier. And from that point on, we were as together as was possible, within the dictates of our lives.

Our relationship was basically a need-based one. He was the first boy with whom I had ever had such an involved relationship. I had little self-confidence and not much self-esteem. I was always tongue-tied. Light conversation was a foreign language to me. Consequently, I avoided most social situations. I clung to him and he built me up until I outgrew him. Yet still we built our dream castles, and I think we might have continued this way if he had not decided to join the Navy.

He had spoken of this often during the two years I'd known him, but somehow I never really thought that he would leave. I viewed it very selfishly as I did many facets of our relationship. I finally faced the fact that our lives were never going to fit together. Already, I had discovered that he was not the only one who would have me. Drunk on my new-found self-confidence and with a somewhat swelled head, I knew that if he left, it would not be long before I found someone else.

So, on a rainy day in November, three months before he was to leave, I told him that I thought it was best that we break up while he was gone. Perhaps when he got back . . . I was still not being totally honest. I had no intention of ever being involved with him again. I already had the beginning of a new relationship. Not long before he left I was living with someone who I now love very much.

For me, it was easy. But for him . . . I saw him often, while I was driving someplace and he was always walking alone or riding a bicycle. If he saw me he might wave or just pretend that he didn't notice me. Occasionally, we might visit, but time would have to pass before we could be friends. I heard from others that he was cynical and bitter. I hadn't realized how his cynicism had faded during those two years we were together.

After he had left for the Navy, he sent me one short letter. After four months I couldn't think of the words to answer him, and before I ever got around to writing a letter, he was killed by a truck while pedalling his bicycle down to the beach on a warm San Diego night.

I remember how he loved the ocean. I would lie on the warm sand listening to the hum of the sky, watching him as he leapt like a dolphin through the surf. Sometimes wading so far out that he was a mere speck. And he would finally run up the beach to me, huffing and blowing, sprinkling me with ice-drops of salt water. And we were in harmony. He and I and some lost summer's day set in my memory like an opal on black velvet.

$\mathcal{F}$og was coming in, thick and cold. The low moist grayness rolled softly over and over, bringing colder air and a dampness akin to rain. Waves began to build up.

The weekend warriors were deserting the beach. Huddled closely in their blankets and coats, they were abandoning their temporary stronghold to the surfers, beachcombers, and lovers of the sea.

I stood, my bare shoulders shivering; it was cold without the protection of my wet suit, but I wanted to feel the water against my skin.

My feet ached with cold as I entered the water. When I reached the first breakline I had to dive through a breaking wave. I tasted the familiar salt water and felt my skin tighten, making a futile effort to preserve the heat of my body against the Pacific. Rising slightly I came out the back of the wave and then eased down into the trough between swells.

I was growing numb; the feeling of cold gradually was replaced by the tingling of rising goose bumps. Soon that, too, would disappear. Head up, using the high arm recovery common to body surfing, I swam toward the outer breakline.

A big wave was building; I could feel its undertow pulling water back from the shore to add to its bulk. So much water had passed me, seaward, that it was shallow enough for me to stand. The swell was coming. Gray water rose above me to the west. I could see its shape changing, the top moving faster than the base; the back moving faster than the front, climbing the swell until it fell crashing over the crest and in front of it; the water at the back racing over and pouring down after the crest until the wave is dissipated in churning white froth.

I should have dived through and slid down the back of the swell; at worst I would have been caught in the edge of the white water, tossed a little on the surface, and dragged toward the beach. But it was too late, the wave would break over me.

To the west and above me the wall of water formed an arc. The world seemed to darken as the sky was blotted out; the arc tightened and I was in a cave of water. The wave tip bent nearer the ocean surface. Time stopped. Water dripped from the curl above me; one drop; six. The wave waited.

Fear tasted dry in my mouth. I could smell the sea odors of salt, iodine, and fish; the sound of waiting roared in my ears. I licked my salty lips and gulped my last air supply against the coming need. My teeth clenched as the dripping water became a curtain.

The top of the wave dropped on me, crashing me to the ocean floor. My body went limp, giving itself to the fury of the sea. I was spun around and around as the water rushing over the crest fell in front of the maelstrom and was pulled back into the churning curl. Sand and pieces of shell, small sea animals joined me, tumbling through the water, under the water. Thousands of tons of water shipped me about, tossing me as easily as a bit of loose seaweed.

My air was giving out; I needed to breach the horizontal whirlpool in order to breathe. I pushed off the ocean floor with all my strength only to find my face scraped along the bottom, stirring up more grit. Crouching against the bottom I thrust with my legs, shooting towards the surface; I hit sand so hard my mouth was filled with it. Lungs bursting, I tried to angle away from the beach, out the back of the white water, but I had no confidence. When all directions lead down, the senses are quickly confused.

Breaking through to the surface, spitting sand from my mouth, I inhaled great gulps of fog. I rinsed my mouth in the salt water of the Pacific and found the taste of it good. By training or instinct I dived through the next breaker. I needed rest. My body rose and fell with the swells. I felt like that primordial being who first prepared to leave the sea; that great adventurer in the evolutionary chain to man.

When the right wave came I was ready. I led it by a short distance, swimming as fast as I could toward the shore. Sneaking a look over my shoulder I saw that I was in the right place. One last arm pull and the wave lifted me toward its crest. Arms at my sides, I held my body rigid with one knee bent, in the posture I've always used. The wave broke, throwing water toward the shore, over its back. I was engulfed in the churning water to my waist; felt the spinning, forward moving power of the water as it poured off my legs and the lower part of my body. My chest and shoulders were free, in front of the wave, and I was held above the surface of the water. Lifting my head cautiously I could see that I was rushing toward the beach as the wave pushed me onward.

The force of the breaker diminished and it set me down gently, surrounding me with bursting white bubbles in the calm water. I swam the remaining distance to the shore.

I realized that I was cold when I stood and walked up the beach. Blood was oozing from my shoulder. Later, when I was warm, it would hurt, but I felt nothing.

Smiling, I spoke to a friend. "Great day! Think the surf'll hold?

"It's gonna be up all day. Stick around!"

*H*arvey called about nine that night and told me the rig was in trouble. He asked if I could meet him at the Red Stack office in San Francisco, where he had a tug boat standing by. I told him I'd be there in about a half hour and grabbed some warm clothes and went out the door.

It probably sounds strange that I didn't even ask what the trouble was, but that was the nature of my work. I had been working for the past two years for a company that specialized in heavy cargo loading, and marine construction, salvage and demolition. In this line of work when someone said a magic word like trouble, help, or hurry, you didn't just sit around asking a lot of questions. All I knew was that we would have to take a boat from San Francisco to Pacifica in order to find out exactly what the trouble was.

Hopefully, when we got to Pacifica we would find a 100-ton capacity crane, mounted on a 50 by 100 foot barge, about a quarter of a mile off the beach. I say hopefully because we hadn't worked the rig that day because of bad weather, and the place it was anchored offered no shelter from the wind or sea.

I remembered the uncomfortable feeling I'd had when Harvey and I and the diving crew anchored the rig about a month ago for this job, which was to replace some damaged sections of an outfall sewer line from Pacifica. To do this we had to place our two stern anchors as close to the beach as possible in order to get close enough to the

36

line to work it. Then we had to place our two bow anchors as far seaward as possible, in order to pull the rig out of the breakers when the weather got bad. The trouble was when we placed our two inshore anchors where we needed them, we didn't have enough wire left on the winch drums to place the offshore anchors where they were needed. Harvey was the crane operator and I was the deck engineer. As such we were theoretically responsible for the safety of the rig. It was a bad situation, but we had managed to get by that way for a month without landing the rig on the beach.

The boat was waiting at the pier when I got to San Francisco. After we got under way Harvey explained that he had just come from Pacifica and had stopped at the beach to look at the rig. He said it looked like one of the offshore anchor wires had broken, because the rig was not lined up with its stern square to the beach as we had left it. If the other offshore wire broke before we got there, we wouldn't be able to do a thing.

As soon as we passed under the Golden Gate Bridge the ocean began to get rough. The farther south we went, the rougher it got. The size of the swells increased until they resembled green mountains, moving silently through the darkness. As each one approached it would bury the bow of the boat under a wall of water. Then the boat would rise to the top and hesitate precariously, only to come crashing down again into the trough where the process would begin again. It made the 60-foot tug boat seem like a child's small toy.

After about two hours of this, the captain announced that he wouldn't take the boat alongside the barge when we got there. It was an old wood-hulled boat, too large to maneuver very fast, and he was afraid he would smash it against the steel hull of the barge. He had some bright idea about Harvey and me dragging a towline over to the barge with a life raft. We vetoed that idea real quick and radioed for our work boat in Half Moon Bay to meet us at Pacifica. It was a small tug with twin engines and a steel hull and was highly maneuverable.

We got to the rig about an hour before the other boat, but all we could do was shine lights on the rig and look at the damage. The forward port anchor wire was gone and the swells were breaking over the deck. The deck had been covered with hatch-boards, but most of them were washed away. What gear was left on deck had been thrown into a pile at the base of the crane. A two-ton clamshell bucket had been knocked over and moved several feet by the force of the waves. The crane's house tiedowns had loosened and we could hear the house as it slammed up and down on its rollers. The one remaining offshore anchor wire was taking a beating, but seemed to be holding well.

After what seemed like hours the work boat got there. Getting from the big tug to the smaller one was a lot easier said than done. If your timing was right you could jump to the other boat as it was on the way up, before the boat you were leaving began to rise with the swell. I jumped first and made it without any trouble. Harvey hesitated too long before he jumped. When he left the big boat it was still rising, but the boat I was on was falling on the backside of a swell. I saw him flying through the air and made an effort to catch him, but my catch turned out more like a tackle and we came down hard on the deck. We both got a few bruises, but it was better than looking for a man overboard in a storm.

When we got to the rig we had to go through the same thing again to get from the boat to the barge deck. It was easier this time, because the barge didn't pitch up and down as bad as the boats.

Once on deck we had to do our work between breakers, holding on to something each time one of them hit to keep from being washed overboard. The hardest part was to get the towing bridle hooked up on the bow bits. Up at the front of the barge we were hit by the full fury of the sea, and it took every ounce of strength we could summon to hold ourselves against each breaker. Again time seemed to stop and the 15 or 20 minutes we spent at the bow of the rig seemed like hours.

38

When the towline was hooked up all that remained was to cut the other three anchor wires, since there was no hope of retrieving the anchors in this weather. The anchors weighed six tons each, and the deck winches weren't powerful enough to drag them in. We scrounged through the debris and managed to get a cutting torch operating. After we got the last wire cut we waved to the boat to haul us home.

After we were on tow and out of the breakers, we cleared the debris from the galley hatch and went below out of the weather. While I started a wood fire in the pot-bellied stove, Harvey got his bottle of Early Times out of its hiding place. I never liked Early Times, but sitting there by the fire, sopping wet and too tired to give a damn, I can't remember whiskey ever tasting so good.

*I*t had been raining and blowing for more than 36 hours, steadily and very hard at times. I reached inside my rain pants, dug into the pocket of my soaked levis, pulled out my watch and saw that it was 6 a.m., straight up. We had been working for 22 hours. The PG&E wires that covered the town like a net seemed like frail cobwebs that the storm had beaten down to the ground. We had just finished putting a 4,000-volt circuit back into operation, and the dispatcher had rewarded us with an easy tag—one customer out of power. The worst it could be was one transformer out of commission.

We neared the location, straining our eyes to find the trouble. The transformer fuses were intact, which meant the transformer was all right. The foreman had spotted the service wires down at the clearance pole. All we had to do was run a new 240-volt service, a simple routine job. Looking again at my watch, I wondered how many more hours we would have to work. Working 22 hours is bad enough in good weather, but with the rain and strong winds it takes twice the effort to do the same job. The truck driver and foreman measured out the wire we needed as I strapped on my hooks and put on my hard hat and safety belt. Once at the top of the pole, I snapped the handline around the cross-arm and waited for the truck driver to send me up the new service wires.

Dawn had broken, the wind was dying down, and the rain was falling softly. I leaned back in my safety belt and relaxed for the first time in three or four hours. It seemed for sure that the storm was weakening, we had an easy routine job, and soon we would be headed for the restaurant to warm up and eat, maybe even to go home to get out of our wet clothes. That bed sure would feel good today.

The clanging of the hook at the top of the handline startled me from my daydream. I took the service wires from the hook and tied them off to the cross-arm. The foreman connected the house end of the wires and gave me the o.k. to hook up my end. I shaped the jumpers and started skinning the ends of the wires when I noticed that I didn't have my rubber gloves with me. I started to have someone send them up to me, but then it would take some time, and there were only three connections to go. I would use my wet leather gloves and be careful not to get in series.

I hooked up the neutral first, and then connected one of the "hot" legs, taking care not to touch both bare wires at the same time. Holding the last service wire in my left hand, I reached with my right hand for the final "hot" jumper.

I was no longer cold and wet, the wind was no longer blowing, the rain didn't exist—all that existed were the two balls of fire that I held in my hands and couldn't get rid of. Every muscle in my body flexed as I pushed the wires away from each other and stretched my arms to get the source of the pain further away from my body. As my muscles contracted my hands came closer to my face; I fought to keep them away.

Then there was no fight, no balls of fire, only the rain touching my face. I looked up and saw the last service wire still not connected—it all flashed back, I had gotten the service wires in series. The truck driver and foreman were yelling up to me, asking if I was all right. I shook my head that I was, not wanting to admit that I felt like I was going to vomit. I somehow suppressed the warm feeling that kept gurgling up in my throat.

One connection to go—no, I was not going to try again with my wet leather gloves. I had tried once and it could have killed me. I was now wide awake and this was no longer a routine job. It was a delicate job that required all my attention and caution. Between the warm tides that rose and ebbed in my throat, I called for my rubber gloves.

*I*t was just another cold, clear winter day, yet men would die and boys would grow old rapidly. In 1944 it was a sign of the times.

I was awakened by a loud voice saying, "Roll out you flyboys, breakfast in 30 minutes." I looked at my watch and it was 3:30 a.m. The fire in the little potbellied stove was long out, and the winter cold had taken over the barracks. It was the beginning of another long day as I lit a cigarette and dressed in wool pants and a shirt, a heavy flight parka, and sheepskin flight boots.

With the other members of our crew I went out into the cold. We had a quarter-mile walk to the mess hall. There were about six inches of snow on the ground, and the sky was crystal clear with that big full moon. The English called it a bombers' moon because they flew at night, and the moon would light their target.

I was 20 years old, a tail gunner, flying in a B-17 bomber with the United States Eighth Air Force stationed in England. I had been flying combat missions for four months, and this was a work day because we flew daylight missions. Breakfast was the same as always— powdered eggs (not very good)—but I ate all I could because we would not eat again until after six that night.

"Your primary target will be Gelsenkirchen," the briefing officer informed us. "It is in the middle of the Rohr Valley, the heart of the German industrial might." We could expect heavy flak on the bomb run. The factories were well protected with 88- and 105-caliber anti-aircraft guns. We would be flying at 29,000 feet and within the range of both types of guns.

I left the briefing, picked up my heated flight suit, parachute, and two 50-caliber machine guns which made up the tail stinger of our bomber, and climbed into a truck. As we rode across the field, the dark silhouettes of the aircraft appeared and were lost in the morning darkness; the moon was now gone. The truck stopped in front of a black silhouette and we climbed out.

Once in the ship I mounted the guns, checked the ammunition, tried the oxygen, electrical, and intercom systems. When I was sure all was ready, I crawled around the tail wheel and walked up to the radio compartment. I asked Charlie, the radio operator, to wake me when we reached the English Channel, then I lay down on the floor and fell asleep.

Someone was kicking my feet. As I opened my eyes, the sun was bright and warm; the roar of the engines reminded me where I was. Charlie said, "Get into the tail and on oxygen; we're at 10,000 feet." I crawled around the tail wheel to the back of the ship, plugged in the heated suit, put on my oxygen mask, and checked the ball to be sure that I was getting oxygen. I called the pilot and reported the tail guns were manned. I was large for a tail gunner and couldn't wear my chest-type parachute, so I placed it on the floor behind me.

The sun was at my back as we were flying east; we crossed the French coast at 15,000 feet. Being the camera ship, we flew number four position. The three ships in front of us were 10 to 15 feet above our ship. They formed a wedge and our ship made the formation a diamond. The other ships of our 12-ship squadron were above, below, and slightly behind us.

The chatter on the intercom was about the weather; it was clear and beautiful. The French countryside looked like a large patchwork quilt of white and gray. This was not a good day for us because the temperature was down to 40° below zero, and the white billowing contrails were pointing to us like arrows. The German gunners could see us coming and did not need their electronic range finders, which we could jam. These gunners were some of Germany's best and used the tracking method; that is, they tracked an individual aircraft with a battery of four guns, and they were damn accurate.

The navigator said that the "I.P." (initial point) was 10 minutes ahead, and we could expect flak in about five minutes. The pilot told me to keep my eyes open and call the flak bursts. The navigator was right: the black mushroom bursts were right on time. I called flak bursts and the pilot took evasive action. Suddenly there was a loud explosion and the ship shuddered; we were falling straight down, left wing first. The right wing was a sheet of angry orange flames. I reached for my chute pack, but the centrifugal force of our fall had glued it to the floor; I couldn't move. As I watched the flames, a B-17 was turning end over end and somersaulted over our right wing tip, forming a ball of fire. The ship in front and above us had been hit between the two engines on the right wing. The wing folded over and crushed the pilot's compartment. The bomber was falling down on top of our bomber, and we both still had a full load of high explosive bombs. Our pilot had put our ship into a vertical bank in an attempt to get out of the way. While we were recovering from the fall, I watched the burning mass. Four chutes billowed out below. The bombs blew! The light was blinding and little black pieces floated toward the ground. There were empty beds in the barracks that night, five permanently.

The pilot had our bomber under control and back in formation as the bombardier called, "Bombs away!" As I watched for the bomb strike I heard the lead pilot radio to disperse until we could clear the flak area. I could see our bombs exploding in the railroad marshalling yard, the primary target area for our bomb group. There must have been ammunition in some of the rail cars because they disintegrated in smoke and fire.

I felt a slight bump and heard the tearing of metal, saw the bright red flash and the black mushroom cloud, and heard the sound of small rocks on our ship's metal skin as a 105 shell passed through the floor, out the roof, and peeled open the front of the vertical stabilizer, before bursting harmlessly above us. My intercom and electrical systems were gone, but I still had oxygen. We were in the combat area so I stayed with my guns. I could feel the added wind from the gaping holes, and I was getting cold. Tom, the waist gunner, came back to check on me and report the damage to the pilot. After about a half hour Tom came for me; the pilot wanted to talk to me. I had to crawl to the radio compartment; my feet were so cold and numb I could not stand or walk.

We were well clear of the target area and on our way back to England when Charlie picked up an American station on the radio; and the news reporter said, "The Eighth Air Force B-17 bombers . . . Today, losses were light."

*P*eter is a teacher of art, and I am one of his students. He is a large man, well over six feet. He has large brown eyes which are mischievous and smiling. He has a prominent nose, some call it a Roman one. Peter's hair is white and lies in duck tails around the sides of his bald top. His hair almost looks like white wings. His chest is full of white and black hair—like a bear. He is moody like a bear.

In the winter he wears tennis shoes and in the summer sandals. He always wears blue jeans. I asked him if he owned a suit and he said he had three of them, but they were all over 20 years old! One was 35. He is not fond of suits; he is more comfortable in his jeans. All of his jeans have large pockets to carry things in. His shirts are all of one pattern—a boat neck with raglan sleeves that have been cut with the main body of the shirt. All of them are striped in neutral shades, in the colors of the earth.

Peter was born and raised in Munich, Germany, and there he went to art school. His family lived down the block from Heinrich Kley, a well-known advertising artist, who was a close friend of Peter's father. Peter's name is Wolfgang Peter, but his mother dropped the Wolfgang when he was young, thinking it too old a name for a young fellow. Peter met and married a young woman from Sebastopol, California, while she was in Germany. She too was studying at an art school. She is beautiful, small, gracious, and quiet. May, Peter's wife, also paints, but she is not so well known as her husband, and she does not teach.

I said he was moody like a bear. He is also affectionate, distant, and friendly. He always surprises me. For example, every 20 minutes our model gets a five-minute rest. One day at every break he would come and sit with me and tell me bits and pieces of his early life. On some days, though, he hardly speaks to anyone.

When I come into class often he will say hello but sometimes he won't. At other times he will give me an affectionate hello kiss. When he is not friendly it does not bother me. Something is on his mind or he is just hungry. We always bring things to eat, and he likes to make the rounds to taste whatever we are eating. He shares his bananas and cups of coffee with us too.

Peter is also a connoisseur of music. He has tapes from every country, from early primitive types of music to contemporary kinds, all of which he plays in class. If we have an African dancer (which we've had), then Peter puts on African music. The music sets the mood for the model and sometimes the mood of our paintings.

Peter and his wife spend every summer in Arizona on one of the Indian reservations. The Navahos are their favorite people, and he spends his time with them out under their hot summer sun painting them. He comes home with hot, rugged paintings of the people and the land. Peter and May both speak Navaho fluently. The Navahos are very close to Peter and sometimes I think he believes he is one.

Peter is very gentle when he teaches. He does not tell you how to do it at first, but he shows you and then he will wipe out what he has done. After he has done this many, many times, you learn by watching him. His criticism is gentle too. He will whisper behind your back and tell you to back away and get a good overall look. If you continue to make the same mistakes as though you were insensitive to his teaching, he will become very angry and, not whispering, he will tell you that you can't draw (if that is the problem) and you will either get out of the class because you have been humiliated and are too proud to take it and learn, or you will learn how to draw.

Peter had always told me quietly how to draw and paint correctly, but one day he corrected me very loudly in front of the whole class. He told me to get a mirror and look at my work backwards, which throws the painting into a whole new perspective and helps you to see the mistakes more easily. I felt terrible because everyone was listening, and it was a horrible insult (you really need help, perhaps more than he can give, if you need a mirror).

Each one of us who stayed had to learn how to take correction from him as well as to learn how to apply it to our work. There are no proud people in his class, because we all have much to learn. Everyone was so kind to me after the scolding, because all of them had received it at one time too.

Peter's earlier paintings were extremely representational and full of detail. Now he is getting looser and more abstract. I think the air, light, and heat of Arizona are coming through.

He is a kind and gentle person, though I wish he would be more open with me. He is very private. Occasionally, however, he gives me secrets that took him 20 or 30 years to learn. He is a generous man.

*M*y brother is one year and two weeks older than me and will be 20 next January. He has blond hair and very bright, piercing blue eyes. His eyes are framed by thick, long, curly lashes and bushy eyebrows. Being slightly near-sighted, he wears glasses. Though glasses distract from some people's looks, I think they add to Ken's. He has a slightly pug nose, thin lips, and a square jawline. I wouldn't say that he's handsome, but on the whole, he is pretty nice-looking. His hair is thick and wavy, and he hates the way it gets bushy when it is wet! My brother is about 5'10", and due to a lot of competitive swimming he has a slender, but quite good, build.

Because we are so close in age and have done and shared so many things together, we are very close emotionally. We were adopted together at the ages of four and five into our present home, where we have really wonderful parents.

Before being adopted, we lived in a foster home and were pretty much our own friends. We played together, fought together, cried together, and laughed together. Though there were other kids living with us, they didn't associate much with Ken and me, so we learned to stick together in most of what we did. We played together in a cowshed, never caring about the dirt and cobwebs, or the cows going in and out. Together, we managed to get ourselves locked into a chicken coop, and of course, blamed each other when asked how we had done it. Together, we compared ideas about "the nice man and lady who took us out to lunch one day and told us they were going to be our mother and father." We agreed that it would be fun living with them and having "real" parents. Together, we squealed and marveled at the stack of coloring books that awaited us in our new home. Of course, we were pretty young at the time, and the material things impressed us immensely. As we grew up, we learned to appreciate more important things, like our home, parents, and friends.

When Ken and I entered elementary school, he was my protector and buddy until he discovered that boys weren't supposed to like girls! Still, Ken ate lunch with me in the cafeteria every day. I think the main reason was because I used to share my lunch with him if he finished before I did!

It was during these times in elementary school, when we were always together, that many people asked us if we were twins, because at the time, we looked pretty much alike. We were both tow-headed, blue-eyed and freckled, and of about the same height.

After elementary school, Ken went to an intermediate school while I was still going to elementary. Then while I was still at intermediate, he entered high school. By the time I, too, was entered in high school, Ken was going through the "cool" stage, and he forbade me to speak to him at school. It was to be a cardinal sin! This was, I think, due to the traumatic experience he had when I passed him in the hall one day and called out "Hi, Kenny!" His friends didn't let him forget it for a long time afterward. After all, he was a big high school sophomore and he went by the name of "Ken"!

Despite many quarrels, fist fights, and general disagreements, Ken and I were still standing by each other for encouragement in dealings with friends and teachers, and in our hobby interests. Our parents always stood by us and gave us encouragement, too, but sometimes we wanted it from someone our own age.

Of course, there were many times when my brother would talk for hours on end about cars and mechanics, and I wasn't very patient about it. He was a typical boy where cars were concerned—always fixing them up or talking about the car he was "going to get."

I guess I never realized how Ken had changed over the years until he started standing on his own two feet, making his own decisions without telling me first, and gradually growing away from me. Last summer my brother went into the Army. At first it was really hard to get used to his being gone. I'd still wake up and peek into his room to wake him up, only he wasn't there. Often I'd find myself still setting the table for four people and going to call him for dinner. By this time, he was interested in outside girl friends, and I was jealous to see that they got letters from Ken much more often than I did. Now, I'm used to his not-so-frequent letters, but I'm awfully happy every time the mailman brings one for me. It's fun to read his "big brother" comments to me. He tells me to take care of myself because "one of these days this brother of yours is coming home on leave, and he'd best find you in good health." It makes me happy that he wants to sound dominating and protective towards me, even though I resent his actually being so.

I haven't seen my brother in a year, but he's coming home; soon, he hopes. I hope so too.

*M*y brother Max died alone in a hotel room in Edmonton, Alberta, at the age of 37. I guess he just went to sleep and never woke up. The doctor that examined his body said his death was caused by a coronary thrombosis, which I understand is a blood clot that blocks one of the main arteries of the heart.

That was two years ago, and when it happened I thought I'd never feel happy again. I've learned that you can't feel sad forever — or at least I can't — but a spark has gone out of my life that I don't think I can replace.

Out of six children Max and I were the closest in age; he was five years older. People said he was the most Jewish looking member of our family, with his thick, curly black hair, dark eyes with horn-rimmed glasses that were forever sliding down a prominent nose, and the olive skin that characterized everyone except mother and me. I had always thought he was handsome, but in retrospect I realize that what I took for good looks was really just a lot of charm.

There were many interesting characteristics of my brother's personality, like he really dug people, and was a flaming, card-carrying Socialist. But the side of him that I could relate to most was Max the Musician.

He really wanted to be a fine jazz musician. He took up alto and tenor sax when he was only 15 and practiced day and night. It seemed in our house we ate, drank, and slept music.

When I was 11 he took me to my first Stan Kenton concert. In those days Kenton had almost every jazz musician of worth in his band. That might be a bit of an exaggeration but consider this list: Shelly Manne (drums), Laurindo Almeida (guitar), Bob Cooper and Art Pepper (tenor and alto), Shorty Rogers and Maynard Ferguson (trumpet). I was only a little girl but I'll never forget what I heard and saw.

This experience started an extended course in music appreciation with Max as my tutor. We used to listen to records by the hour. If a solo by a particular musician was good, Max would pick up the turntable arm and repeat and repeat it, then he'd say, "Now sing it for me." I have jazz riffs still running through my head that I learned years ago.

My brother was deeply moved and excited by Charlie Parker. He used to say that the Bird could express every kind of emotion with his horn. It was like he used his instrument to communicate feelings for which there were no words. I remember once when we were listening to a Parker side that was cut shortly after he'd been released from a mental hospital (he was a drug addict), and he sounded so lonely, sad, and lost that he made Max cry. I too wept.

Max used to say that most people listen at music and not to it. I think that's his legacy to me — the gift of appreciation through listening and understanding.

At his memorial service, his friends gathered together and played his favorite records and talked about him and told what knowing him had meant to them. A few guys brought their horns and jammed a little. To outsiders I'm sure it would have appeared to be an irreligious event.

*M*y father was a short, slightly built man who didn't seem to mind that nearly everyone was taller than he, even his children when they got to be about 11 years old, and most noticeably my mother who was not only taller and heavier, but bigger in the way that she expressed her endless opinions.

He often let people have the upper say, not because he was timid, but simply because he lacked the know-how for verbal battle. Being a completely fair-minded person, he understood how some people felt it necessary to let off steam every once in a while. Certain people more often than others. On those occasions, he would just sit and fend off words with determined quietude, and then calmly and with dignity far in excess of his stature, he would tell those concerned the way he wanted things done, and with very few exceptions, things were always done his way.

My father had a friend who came from the same town in Hungary as he did. His name was Sam Meislik and he was very tall, over six feet at least. Sam was also a Jew and a constant aggravation to my mother who said that it wasn't normal for Jews to be tall and it wasn't right for my father to be friendly with someone who wasn't normal. This didn't bother Sam or my father in the least. They went about their friendship, patiently putting up with the woman who was unfortunately burdened with so many disapprovals.

Just before the depression, Sam and my father invested in an apartment house. It was one of the many things they did together. When the depression hit, they lost the house, along with almost everything else they owned. This further added to my mother's conviction that they wouldn't have lost the house, indeed, there wouldn't have been a depression at all, if Sam had not been a Jew.

Shortly before I was born, my father bought a small house in the Bronx. It had a large backyard and a huge basement that offered many possibilities for another partnership venture between my father and Sam. They no longer had the money to go about it in a big way, but the incentive to do something together was still there, so they decided to try their hand at wine-making. They had an added advantage this time, because my mother was now busy evoking a maternal instinct in herself and no longer had the time or inclination to pin-prick tall Jews and other things.

Since not much money was involved, they couldn't go wrong no matter what they did. Even when the wine wasn't drinkable, it made great vinegar. And when it was bad vinegar, it still was a wonderful way for a couple of old friends who were too foreign for baseball and too domesticated for carousing to spend their weekends.

Even when the wine-making season was over, Sam came every Saturday and Sunday to see my father. They would sit on the front porch then and talk, mostly about how things used to be in the old country. Or when the weather was warm, they would walk to Bronx Park which was near where we lived, and which had paths through the woods that reminded them of the forests in Hungary. Or Sam would help my father with whatever fixing-up or painting he had to do around the house.

My father was a carpenter by trade and worked in, of all places, Rupert's Brewery. It's hard to imagine what a carpenter does in a brewery, but my father did it and with a great deal of pride, too. He talked often about his job and showed much concern for business conditions and for the men who worked with him. Sam was a tailor and he worked for Weber & Heilbroner, a men's clothing store in

Manhattan. To hear them tell it, they had the two most important jobs in the two best companies in the country.

Sam had a wife, only I never met her. He always came alone to visit us, and she apparently didn't mind him spending so much time at our house. My mother never asked him to bring her, probably because my mother didn't care much for the company of other women and least of all for Sam's wife. Eventually my mother gave up trying to separate Sam and my father. This was the only time that I've known her to admit defeat. She also came to accept Sam and his friendship for its true value, and in the time after my father's death gave up her prejudices and relied almost completely on him for consolation and financial advice.

My father died two years before Sam in October, 1951, at about the time the wine would have been fermenting had he and Sam worked the grapes that year.

$\mathcal{I}$t all started about seven years ago when my mother-in-law, a woman about five feet tall and a little on the plump side, began to have severe stomach pains. Having always been in generally good health, she thought it was just something she had eaten which didn't agree with her. After a time, however, she began to vomit after eating. This turn of events sent her to a doctor for an examination. After the doctor had performed some preliminary tests, he immediately sent her to the hospital for exploratory surgery.

On the day she was scheduled for surgery, I was working in my office when the phone rang. It was just before noon. My wife was on the line, crying as I had never heard her cry before or since. I knew something terrible had happened. Through her sobs I could make out that she wanted me to come to the hospital. One of the men I work with was in my office at the time, and upon seeing my plight he offered to drive me to the hospital.

All kinds of thoughts raced through my head. I dared not think of the worst. When we finally reached the hospital, I ran up the cement stairs leading to the hospital entrance. My wife was at the opposite side of the hospital grounds. As she turned to face me I could see she was still crying. She rushed to me and threw herself into my arms. It took what seemed forever to get her quieted down enough so she could tell me what was wrong. Finally she managed to blurt out that the surgeon had opened her mother up and found cancer, incurable. There was nothing to do but close her back up and wait for the inevitable. I couldn't believe it, or rather didn't want to believe it. A woman who loved life and even more, loved her only grandchild, our son, like life itself, was to have her own life snuffed out so soon.

She was released soon after to pick up her life as best as she could in the few months the doctor had given her. Being the strong-willed woman she was, she hung on tenaciously for two years. In those years we watched her life ebb away. Her body shrank to a mere shadow of what it used to be, and her large, sparkling, laughing eyes grew dim and full of pain. We never heard her complain. She soon was unable to care for herself or be cared for by her husband, and she was placed in a convalescent hospital.

When we went to visit her, I couldn't help but notice what an imposing building the hospital was. All brick and glass with well-kept lawn and shrubs. Upon entering the lobby I could see a beautiful water fountain surrounded by flowers. A sitting room with fireplace and large TV set. In the sitting room I could see several old people. Some were in wheelchairs, some on crutches, and some were helped along by a hospital attendant. No one was smiling. It appeared as though they were just waiting for their time to come to leave this world. We went down the corridor, hearing only the noise our shoes made on the shiny linoleum. As we turned into my mother-in-law's room we could see her bed. There sticking out from underneath the covers was her head, with sunken eyes and loosely falling skin. A mass of gray hair stuck out in disarray. She said to me, "How are you, Harvey?" That's the way my mother-in-law was, always concerned about everyone but herself. We didn't stay very long.

The next day I got a phone call from my father-in-law. He said in a voice trying not to cry, "It's all over, mother is gone." For a moment I couldn't think of what to say. Finally I replied I would come to the hospital. As I walked into the hospital this time, I didn't notice the fountain or the sitting room, nor did I see any people present. I could only hear silence as I walked down the corridor. I approached the room in which my mother-in-law was confined, and I saw an attendant wheel her body, covered with a sheet, out into the hall. I stopped and turned aside and began to cry. I cried partially from sadness and partially from relief, for now her suffering was finally over.

I had decided early in my second pregnancy that the birth process this time would include participation from me, not just from nurses, doctors, and attendants, who except for my family doctor would be total strangers to both my baby and me.

The impersonal, antiseptic way they had delivered my first child had been for some time a source of irritation to me. The medics had claimed that I had "helped" and that I was a good little pusher, to which I felt like saying what on earth else can your body do when an 8½-lb. child wants to be born! But I really remember very little of the whole ordeal with Laura, except that it was an ordeal. Every time a severe contraction came some white-masked nurse would clamp a black rubber mask on my face, and I'd briefly fade into oblivion. Later, much later, they brought a clean, oiled, powdered, fully dressed little girl to me, and I thought, God, I hope she's mine and they haven't picked up the wrong baby by mistake. I had been left so totally out of the whole experience, how could I tell? At 18, however, you don't have the nerve to criticize the medical priesthood.

Three years later when I discovered that I was pregnant again, I suffered from no such loss of nerve. I clearly explained my feelings to my doctor (same one), and I told him that I wanted natural childbirth and rooming-in with this baby, and if he or the hospital refused I'd simply have the child at home in my own bed and call in a midwife as my mother and grandmother had done. To my astonishment he totally agreed with my philosophy and said he'd see what he could do to override the hospital rules.

I eagerly began attending a small natural childbirth class that had been started in the basement of a nearby church. It was given by a group of nurses and encouraged by a progressive (or old-fashioned?) group of doctors that wanted childbirth to return to being a more joyful event. The classes were free and the emphasis was on correct breathing during labor, and exercises to instruct the mother how to relax certain muscles during labor contractions. The idea being that if you learn your lessons well, the birth experience can be surprisingly painless. I attended these classes for many months. I don't remember now after so many years what these exercises were called, but I suspect they were pretty much like the LaMaze method popular today.

When the day of birth arrived I was totally prepared psychologically for what was ahead. My doctor had arranged to have a little crib, diapers, and appropriate needs moved into a small private room at the hospital. When I arrived already well along in labor, I was put for a period of time in the labor room. This room contained four beds, two empty and two with women in different stages of labor. They were moaning and groaning, and one of them, the younger, broke into tears from time to time. It occurred to me that she was scared to death. I was really very calm, busily practicing my exercises. Very soon I was moved to a gurney and from there lifted onto the delivery table. The orderlies did this with such ease that I was amazed, since I was the size of a baby blimp. The contractions were coming hard and fast now and the action really began. My doctor had done as he'd promised and hung a mirror over the end of the delivery table.

I was fascinated by the view of myself on the mirror above me. I had dilated to the point where the baby's head was coming through, and the doctor commented that he/she was going to be a big one, and to aid the shoulders now struggling to push out we'd better do a small episiotomy. He used a little local anesthetic and I watched him snip me with scissors. From then on it was rapid, as labor goes. Once the baby was out, the doctor laid her on my somewhat flattened belly and proceeded to cut and tie the cord. I was amazed at how long the cord was, and how bloody and slimy my daughter looked. As a matter of fact she looked really horrible, but I thought she was wonderful and said so loudly to all around. I expelled the afterbirth, and all at hand went to work to clean up my baby, me, and the table.

I can't describe my feeling of elation as they wheeled me back to my little room. The nurse told me to rest, to which I said, "Rest, hell, bring me my baby, I feel marvelous. I will sleep when she sleeps." They brought her in diapered and wrapped in a blanket. I held her to my breast to see if she would nurse, which she did immediately. It was thrilling to hold her and feel her warm round body close to me while she sucked energetically, knowing exactly what to do.

I stayed in the hospital seven days. We had a lovely time, Leslie and I. I bathed her, diapered her, fed her whenever she was hungry. I had no brisk nurse to sweep her away after an insufficient feeding, to return four hours later with a baby purple from crying and again too exhausted to nurse further. I held Leslie for hours, during which time we had long "talks" and got to be fast friends. By the time our week was up I was strong enough to cope with her three-year-old sister and her musician father who kept the strangest hours. I was ready to face housework, dirty laundry and all, with renewed energy and reverence for life.

My mother was sick and she tried to kill herself. We probably should have taken her to the hospital a few days earlier, but it was hard to tell whether she was getting better or worse.

For the past week she had been awake all of the time, night and day. She would lie in bed in the dark but wouldn't sleep. When she did get out of bed, she would wander aimlessly around the house, staring at people in a way uncommon for her. My father told me she came into my bedroom one night and stood by my bed, watching me sleep.

I was in charge of helping her figure out her pill schedule while my father was at work. As long as I could remember she had taken pills, but now she couldn't remember which pills to take, or if she had already taken them. I gave her the right pills at the right times and prevented her from taking the wrong ones at the wrong times.

One afternoon my older sister and her husband came over to see mother and to keep me company. My mother was in the bedroom, supposedly sleeping, and the three of us were watching television and laughing at the stupidity of the shows TV had to offer.

My mother's room connects with the kitchen which in turn connects with the living room. From where we were sitting, I could hear my mother walking around in the kitchen making noises like she was pouring pills from a bottle. The three of us in the living room looked at each other for a second, and then I jumped up and half ran to the kitchen where, sure enough, Mother was standing with a pile of pills in her hand.

I didn't say anything for what seemed like a long time. "It's not time to take your pills," I finally said. She just looked at me as if she was going to cry. "Here, let me put them back because it's not time to take them," I said, holding out my hand to take the pills. She stood looking at me, not saying a thing.

Finally she spoke. "You want me to die."

I got pretty mad at this, replying, "I do not! What makes you say that?" She didn't answer and we both stood there looking straight into each other's eyes for a long time. She spoke again. "You want me to die, I heard you all laughing at me."

"We weren't laughing at you," I said, "we were laughing at the television program — and we don't want you to die." I reached out my hand to take the pills, but she wouldn't give them to me.

"Mom, I love you and I don't want you to die," I said, almost crying. "You're imagining things and I don't like it, because you put words in my mouth and thoughts in my head that aren't there." Finally she opened her hand and I took the pills. I got her to lie back down in bed again, and I returned to the living room to sit with the others.

Once I returned, no one said anything. It was strange; the whole time I was in the kitchen with my mom, I had expected someone to come in and take hold of the situation — both my sister and brother-in-law were older and might know how to handle things better. But no one came in.

When my dad came home I explained everything that had happened, and he went in the room to talk to my mother. Suddenly, we heard him yell something from the bedroom. I went in, and my father looked at me like he was about to cry and said, "We're taking her to the hospital." "What happened?" I asked. "She tried to cut her wrists with the staple remover," he said. "You get her things together and I'll call the hospital."

He went into the next room to call, and closed the door behind him. When he came out again his eyes were red and his voice was a little shaky and I knew he had been crying. I tried to help my mother pack, but she kept insisting that she didn't want to go and she'd unpack what I had just put in her suitcase. Finally we got things together and the three of us got into the car (my sister and her husband had decided to leave). It was just my mother, father and I driving to the hospital on a cold, dark night.

We went to the county hospital where expenses aren't so high. Mom has been in and out of hospitals for the past 10 years, including a stay at the Napa State Hospital for the mentally ill.

Upon entering the waiting room at County, we found we would have to wait for quite a while. The room was big and full of people: girls who were going to have babies, and a tall, black man sitting in a small chair drunk and playing with little kids, and two teenyboppers calling boys on the pay phone and giggling to each other, and a Hell's Angel with a dirty denim jacket and jet black hair combed back, and my mom sitting in a chair trying to cut her wrists on the edge of a coin purse.

Finally, after about an hour and a half they called for her and gave her a five-minute examination, after which they assigned her to a room in a special ward for the mentally ill. We left her suitcase with the nurse and saw her to bed in a room with a small plate of glass in the door for observation.

Within two weeks my mother was back home again and "normal." Nobody knows what caused her to get sick and nobody knows what made her better. But it must be an awfully lonely world when a person feels that everyone in it wants you to die.

$\mathcal{I}$t was what I would have called a normal summer Sunday. I was at my church which is on the outskirts of town, right up the hill from the city golf course. This was a fairly good location for a church, because it wasn't directly surrounded by houses, although there was a tract of homes across the field. But the noise from the children playing outside never reached the other side of the field to our church. So we always had a quiet, serene setting with only the winds of nature raising a disturbance.

On this day, I was taking care of the nursery, something I did whenever I didn't feel like sitting in the church for the hour of sing-ing, reciting, and listening. The nursery is actually the kitchen of our church, and it is right down the hall from the church portion of the building. There is no kind of sound-proofing throughout the kitchen, hall, or church. So any moderate noise is heard quite clearly by everyone, including our pastor, who made it known he doesn't like disturbances, especially during his sermon. My job was to keep the nursery noise down to a soft whisper—a very challenging task.

This morning there were eight very restless children sitting around the kitchen table, looking at me quite innocently while they clut-tered, chattered, and clattered away. I tried games, puzzles, pleas and threats, but the children just continued on. The only answer I could think of was to move the "party" outside where the children could run around and use their energy without disturbing the congregation and pastor very much. So I opened the back door wide and let them loose.

It was really beautiful outside. The weather was mild and there was a breeze that swept across the hill making the tall wild weeds wave like a golden sea. It was so peaceful as I sat there watching that I almost didn't hear the excited screaming of the children. They were pointing emphatically towards the sky, and when I looked in the direction of their waving hands I saw a huge air balloon, like that of the Wizard of Oz, flying freely through the sky. I watched the balloon as it swayed with the brisk breeze and remembered that there was supposed to be a balloon race in the next town, about six miles away. Just as I was wondering why it was the only balloon up in this area, I saw the balloon start to toss around, and it then took a sudden dive into the surrounding telephone wires, exploded into flames and then disappeared behind the hill.

Everything after that happened so fast—but I guess it always seems that way when you see something terrible happening and you know there's not much you can do to help. But I had to do something, so I had one of the older children take the others inside and I then ran down the hill as fast as I could go. As I ran I saw a pickup truck barreling down the road towards the golf course. By the time I got to the burning wreckage of the balloon, the people in the truck were already there. There were two men who were pulling the burning clothing off the pilot who lay near the collapsed balloon. Standing a few yards away was a woman who looked as if she were in a mild state of shock, if not worse. I went to her and asked her if I could do anything. She answered that they had already alerted the police and an ambulance when her husband started going off course. As soon as she said that I heard the sirens, and I started praying that they would get him to the hospital in time.

But as I looked up to see the oncoming cars, I literally couldn't believe my eyes. In all the excitement I didn't hear the gathering of curious onlookers. The field surrounding us and the road leading to the scene were engulfed with people (children and adults) trying to get a good look at what all the excitement was about. But their idle curiosity turned dangerous when they wouldn't move from the road, even for the police cars and ambulance. They simply stood there like zombies. I looked to the woman and saw her crying as she watched these people jeopardizing her husband's life. I slowly felt a feeling of disgust coming over me.

The police slowly cleared the road and had the ambulance go on through while they tried their best to keep the area cleared. But their cries and demands of "clear the road, go home—it's under control, you're in the way," didn't faze the crowd. When the ambulance tried to pass through the crowd again, the people refused to move aside. But this time the driver persisted and simply drove through them. But I already had the feeling that it was too late. And I knew that if the man did die, his death would be the fault of all these people, or at least it would be in my mind.

But I found I could be shocked even more. After the ambulance left, most of the adults started to disperse. Their offspring, however, lingered for one last look. The two men were hurrying to load the torn balloon and basket into the back of their truck. They then helped the young woman into the cab and started down the road towards the gathering of children. Most of the children stayed off the road, but the driver didn't want to chance going faster than 5 or 10 mph, for fear of one of them running out into the roadway.

As the truck slowly rolled along, the young ones scampered and scurried along with it. Then I saw a boy of about nine years old jump up onto the back of the truck, take a small knife and cut pieces off the balloon. He jumped down victoriously and started handing out the pieces to his friends. I felt myself tremble with a feeling of utter disbelief, and I just turned and ran back to the church as fast as I could. And to this day I can't bear to go to the scene of an accident for fear of seeing these destructive curiosity-seekers again.

When I awoke at 6 a.m. on the morning of April 23, 1961, a strange feeling came over me when I thought of what lay ahead that day. I had gotten up early that morning in order to see a man get his last wish. That wish was to die in the gas chamber at San Quentin Prison. I did not know this man, he was just a name. However, I did know why he had been sentenced to death. As I made preparations to leave the house, I considered why I was going and what my reactions would be. I had toured San Quentin earlier in the year in a group, and we had been shown the little five-sided green room known as the gas chamber. I could picture the two empty chairs with numerous straps neatly folded around them, and how the whole room seemed so very clean. Now one of those chairs would have a man sitting in it.

That man would be a 32-year-old Caucasian named Milton Cooper. He had been tried and convicted of rape and murder in one of the Bay Area counties. Cooper had turned down all attempts by his attorney to appeal the conviction, and had written a personal letter to then Governor Edmund Brown asking him not to stay his execution. He told Brown his only wish was to die, and if denied this he would kill again.

I drove alone to Richmond where I picked up another deputy, and as we drove across the Richmond–San Rafael bridge neither of us had much to say. Our anxiety was getting to us. According to the letter of instructions, we had to be at the prison by 8:30 a.m. When we reached the gate it was cool and a light overcast covered the sky. At the gate our car was inspected and we had to check our sidearms, after which we were given directions on where to park. There were extra guards on duty at the gate, and no inmates could be seen working out in the open. We walked to a ramp where we had to remove everything from our pockets and then pass through a metal detector. After clearing this security, we proceeded to the main office where a waiting room had been set up for the witnesses. After all 20 arrived, our names were read off by an official of the prison. Several uniformed guards came into the room, and they instructed us about security measures, the execution schedule, and what was expected of us.

At 9:40 a.m. we were ordered to line up outside in a column of twos. Then, flanked by guards on all sides, we were marched approximately three blocks to a small pentagon-shaped building which was connected to a large cell block. There were more guards standing in front of the large steel door leading into the building. The door was opened for us, and we had to sign a register. Immediately on entering our eyes went directly to the green-colored chamber. The three sides facing us were all windows, and they appeared to be extra clean. There was a guard inside the chamber apparently making some adjustments. Several others could be seen behind a window separating us from the cell block. When we were all inside, they told us a guard would be stationed at the door we had just come through, and to go to that door if we became sick or wanted out. There was no talking among the witnesses, but you had the feeling each was trying to read the others' minds. The associate warden could be seen standing by a telephone, inside the cell block. We were told it was a direct line to the governor's office in Sacramento. The warden kept glancing at it, as if he thought it was going to ring.

The two chairs in the chamber, located side-by-side, reminded me of outdoor sports arena seats, except for the bigger arm rests and the numerous straps still neatly folded. I could see a small bucket of water sitting on the floor directly below a metal lever connected in some way to a series of levers and handles on the outside of the chamber. Someone was testing the device.

The silence was broken by the clanging of metal doors, and a guard entered from the cell block and stood behind the right chair. My eyes turned to a clock, which said 9:55. A tall, slender man dressed in a white shirt without tie, blue trousers, and black shoes walked into the chamber alone. Two guards were behind him. Someone in our group said, "That's Coop." After entering the chamber, Cooper stood for a moment, caught the eye of someone he knew, waved and winked at the person. As he sat in the chair he continued to look out the window, smiling and again winking. Then he mouthed the words "Good-bye." His attention was distracted by the entrance of the prison doctor who attached a stethoscope around his chest and another to his left leg above the ankle. After this was done, the guard standing behind the chair placed the straps across Cooper's arms, chest, and legs. With this done, Cooper again smiled. The guard left the chamber and the stethoscope wires were connected through the door, which was then closed and sealed.

It seemed an eternity while all this had taken place, but a glance at the clock showed it to be 10:03. There was silence in the room, and several witnesses including me looked toward the small window where the associate warden stood by the phone, still with a look of anticipation on his face. There appeared to be a noticeable nod of his head, and at the same time there was the sound of metal striking metal, and all eyes turned to the man sitting in the chair, who with his eyes closed was gasping for air and straining against the straps which held him. After what seemed forever, a smile appeared on his face and his head slowly lowered until his chin rested on his chest. There was some movement among the witnesses, and the guard opened the door and two from our group left.

The small door leading to the cell block opened and the prison doctor appeared and read a statement which said: "The cyanide was dropped at 10:04 and subject Cooper was pronounced dead at 10:09 a.m. April 23, 1961." We were then told to file out and sign the witness forms.

As we came out into the yard the sun was out bright, and its warmth took away some of the gloom. I had witnessed an execution, a man's last wish. It was a day I'll never forget.

I always knew that I had made it, that everything was taken care of for the rest of my life, that no matter what happened, I'd never be sorry that it had happened. Even more, that I was the one that had made it happen in the first place. There were many times like this when I recognized who I was.

One of the flashes I had was in Hawaii. We slept on the beach at night and lay around in the sand and sun during the day, playing and living good. One night my friend Mike and I found a spot to sleep in someone's backyard, right next to the beach. We had gotten settled and I was lying there meditating when I felt this weird cold feeling come over me — it was like death. I had had experiences like this one before but never so intense. I got into session with myself — I didn't open my eyes and with all my power I got through it. A light came into my mind, and I smiled and went to sleep.

The next morning Mike wasn't around. I looked toward the other side of the island and began watching the dark, heavy, rain clouds start evaporating as the sun came up. I watched for about half an hour, then all of a sudden the sky became a giant mirror and I could see the whole island and everything else in the universe. I saw Mike walking back from a hike. He was on a road leading into town some four or five miles away. I decided to go to meet him.

As I approached the town a young girl stopped me. She said, "Don't you ever get tired of knowing everything?" I thought for a moment and then answered, "It has never even occurred to me before," and went on to meet Mike.

He saw me about a quarter of a mile away and waved, glad to see me. When we met he told me that a man had come up to him during the night and put a gun to his head, threatening his life. Some people sleeping down on the beach had seen what was going on and they ran the man off.

$\mathcal{T}$he sun is very warm today, and lying in its warmth I close my eyes to find myself in a purple room with red carpets and a yellow ceiling. The walls are filled with psychedelic posters that make one aware of warmth and "neoninity," like one experiences in Reno on a warm Nevada night.

The walls slowly expand forcing gaps several feet wide to open in the corners, and the ceiling changes hue and fades to the azure coloration of the sky. There is a vastness outside which quietly and slowly eliminates all realization of walls — maybe they crumbled into nothingness or blended into the background, but they are gone. There are forests filled with the wild colors of flowers, the sounds of birds, and the inner darkness that foliation exemplifies. My bare feet are on soft grass still dewy from a damp winter night. Dew that will soon evaporate to fill the atmosphere with moisture in preparation for tomorrow.

Music plays in the background, loud, very hard rock. The sky is not blue as it once was, but red, and the sun does not radiate heat, but energy, and I am filled with vitality and life because of it. I am running across a meadow which materializes from nowhere, jumping over streams that suddenly appear. I am not running with the wind, I *am* the wind!

I love it here. I can feel love radiating from my body and, more importantly, from my soul. Animals appear from nowhere. Smiling at me, they know they are completely safe in my presence — in reality I am no more than an animal myself. A bird flies and lands on my shoulder to whisper something in my ear — *Be Aware! Be Aware!* The words reverberate in my ear and head like so many acoustically imperfect auditoriums where echoes of three beats ago never catch up to reality.

I slow down as a grove of trees appears — a path looms ahead. The entrance is guarded by two lions that strobe between marble and reality, as if they were trying to decide whether to let me enter or not. As I am drawn toward them they roar, *Be Aware! Be Aware!*

As I pass through, everything becomes brighter — reds, blues, and greens are fluorescent. I am in a tunnel as the foliage engulfs me in its majesty. Before me, far in the distance, is a bright light — so bright I must shade my eyes and blink to focus. *Be Aware! Be Aware!* It is merely a pinpoint, but so bright that it must be the sun itself.

As I grope my way, I can feel colors and textures of foliage and the softness of grass as it tickles between my toes. I listen to sounds of nature — the wind whipping a spruce or whistling through a pine or wailing through a weeping willow. The foliage is turning to stone and the trees are becoming buildings — skyscrapers that block out the sky so that I am still in that tunnel.

Always there is that bright light that I am being drawn to, now the size of a golf ball, drawing me as a magnet draws a metallic fragment. I'm moving at a fantastic speed — everything is becoming a blur. Huge buildings are only a minute reflection of time. Blurs of people seem to be talking to me, yet I'm not listening, nor answering, for they are merely reflections of myself, and I never talk to myself.

The light is getting larger. Suddenly I *am* aware of what it is, and I reach out to touch the hand of God.

$\mathscr{F}$or a minute I stop and reason with myself. It is just a dream, I'm in my room, in my bed, and it's three o'clock Wednesday morning and everything is fine. It was just a bad dream.

But then I think about what had seemed so real. The heads in the cupboards that fell down on the counters and floor when I opened the doors. And the eyes, those sunken, waterless, staring eyes! How they stare! When I move about the kitchen they watch me, shifting their eyes, following every step. When I turn quickly the eyes follow me with such force that the heads fall on their sides and roll around on the floor getting specks of food and dust on them. Then the eyes get all bloodshot and blood gushes from them flooding the floor. There is no place to go but up on the table to get out of the red sea of blood. But it looks so high. Can I ever make it up?

As I climb I feel hands pulling on my feet. Not on just two feet though, I have many feet, about six or seven. They all want to step on different chairs, not doing what I want them to, and they almost make me lose my balance and fall.

When I finally get to the top of the table, I find it is so crowded with dishes and food there is hardly room for me. I try not to step on the food or get the tablecloth dirty, but I have no control over all my feet, they have no feeling in them.

Now I look around the table and I see people sitting on the plates.

They have their heads in their hands and are looking and laughing at me. I wonder why. Is it because of all my legs, or maybe they can see all the fear in my eyes? I know it must show. I can't stand all these heads, staring eyes, and all of the blood. That must be why they're laughing at me. What's so funny about fear? I should be the one laughing at them, they're the ones that have lost their heads! But I don't laugh. I can't.

I am staring in a mirror. The image it reflects is ugly to me. The eyes, small and narrow, the rest of the face puffed out of proportion. No real shape exists but a longish fat blob. I stare until the face dissolves and I am looking at the mirror and the world behind it. It's exactly like my room, only it's turned around. Strains of music come from the record player. I begin to dance. I am a ballerina, and I am beautiful. My hair is long and thick and pulled back from my forehead to expose delicate features. I dance a dance I learned as a child. The music heightens, I jump and spin around, calling on every muscle of my body and all my coordination to come to my aid. A change in tempo, I stop short making a good accent, then, with the change in the music again, I fall with the grace of a tinkling waterfall. On the floor I see, reflected in the tiles, the fireplace in the corner. The logs are burning and flickering alive with the flames. I smile at the thought that they look as graceful as I. My head rises and I look down again. My face is in the tiles. Horrid and grimacing it looks, with a smile on its lips. "No!" I choke, and watch as the words mimic themselves in the image. Tears start to fall, trying to obliterate the face in the tiles. They cover all but one puffy eye which blinks in its redness. The black tile becomes a muddy pool, and I, a piglet wallowing in all my glory, lie upon that mud and slime. In this state, I am happy. I am like everyone else. There is no discrimination. All my friends have snub noses, wrinkled pink skin, and tiny, floppy ears.

Ahhh! Ecstasy! The mud is warm and friendly. It oozes about my
back and squishes up by the sides of my head. It's like a warm bath.
I roll over to immerse my stomach in the same feeling. I look down
to put my snout in the goosh. I stop short to see the shimmering mud
reflect a pig's face. The holes of my nose turn into freckles in this
mirror, and the fat face of the pig becomes my own. I watch, and
my mouth gapes open at the grotesqueness of myself. Long stringy
hair hangs from either side of the face. The eyes are so small, I can
hardly see them, so I look closer. I can barely see the brownness of
my eyes which looks like the slime in which I am lying. The whites
of my eyes grow larger. They glare and make me blink. They are the
whole of the picture, and they are so bright my eyes begin to hurt.
I blink rapidly and I can feel the tears form. I look quickly away,
then realize that I am staring at the sun. In one hand, I am holding
a rag, and in the other, polishing wax. A car waits beside me, so I
begin to polish it. I am very proud of this car because it is my own.
She is beautiful, sleek, and long. I run my fingers along her side
feeling the smoothness of her body. Everything about her is perfect,
even the interior. Her color is baby blue, and there is not a scratch or
dent in her whole exterior. She is flawless. I polish some more and
notice in her shine the ugly cars around her. There is a putrid green—
colored one, several burnt-orange cars, and one hideous-looking red
car. The grille on it looks like a smile. I polish the reflection of the
red car, laughing to myself that maybe that will improve the looks
of it, when I notice that it moves when I move. It is my face again,
with my forehead stretched around the curve of the car's front
fender. My eyes are small and placed high upon my forehead. My
nose and mouth are drawn down close to my chin. There is nothing
in the middle of my face, save the beginning of two fat cheeks and a
mass of ugly freckles. This time anger wells up inside of me. Even
though this red face that stares back at me is grossly stretched out of
shape, I know it is my own and I know that I look like that. I scream
with a rage that I hope God can hear. A sledgehammer lies beside me.

I pick it up and smash the face that is mine. I smash it until the paint chips off so the eyes can't stare and the mouth can't grin. I smash it until it will never show its sickening self in my presence again. Sweaty and hot I sink exhausted to the ground, chips of paint strewn around me. I begin to look up, to see what damage I have done in my frenzy, and there, in the hubcap on the wheel, is my face, sitting atop the shoulders of my slumped, fat body, grinning.

PINEGROVE
PRIMITIVE
BAPTIST CHURCH
PASTOR - ELD. J.H. THROWER
MEETINGS EVERY 4TH. SAT. NIGHT, AND SUNDAY
3301

$\mathcal{T}$o me, a ritual is a sociological act evolving within a society in which people participate or refrain from in order to achieve recognition and acceptance from the group. Perhaps rituals, like everything else, run in cycles: old ones re-emerging, present ones fading away for a time. The reason for the ritual may be hazy at best. We might not know where or how it started or who started it, but we do it because it's always been done that way and everybody's doing it.

Now, for what seems like always, I have been cursed with the uncomfortable combination of tender skin and tough, dense whiskers, and since the tender age of 17 I have participated in a daily ritual indulged in by nearly all the males of our society. Shaving! It was never a pleasant five minutes of personal grooming. It was always 30 minutes of minor surgery. After a hot facial soaking or better yet a steamy shower, I would begin the four-step operation: lather, scalpel, rinse, suture.

Somehow, the act of dragging an unbelievably sharp blade across the throat, under the nose, and around a cleft chin began to seem a bit masochistic and silly to me. After years of painstakingly slicing away yards of facial hair, people would walk up to me and say, "Steve, you have 5 o'clock shadow and it's only 9 a.m." Stuff like that. The poor helpful souls didn't realize that I had just stumbled out of the bathroom 60 minutes before with 40 bloody little pieces of toilet paper clinging to my face.

Well, this got to be a routine occurrence to which I never adjusted. The more I shaved the sorer I got. I began to toy with the idea of growing a beard, a ritual of past centuries that was now returning in popularity. After all, if I was blessed with a permanent chinful of 5 o'clock shadow, why not let it grow around the clock?

Why waste 30 minutes a day making my face hurt?

Why waste 20 gallons of water a day to wash away a teaspoon of stubble and foamy? (I always leave the water running not only to rinse the razor, but to drown out the sound of razor grating against protesting whiskers. Sort of like screeching your fingernails across the blackboard just right.)

An electric razor? No way. I tried them all. Rotary types, reel types, all types, and just like lawnmowers they left a little protruding above the surface—through the accompanying rash.

Well, the advantages far outweighed the disadvantages, so for the past three years I have performed the ritual somewhat modified; five minutes to shave around the edges and an occasional scissors trim. I balk even at this, but I can't ignore social realities entirely, nor do I wish to look like Wolfman, which would surely happen if I let it all hang out.

With this one I have reached a reasonable compromise. Next ritual please!

$\mathcal{I}$ think that I have always been a very lonely person. My life actually doesn't amount to very much, but then whose does when one thinks on a universal scale? I haven't traveled the world and tasted exotic food. I've never scaled Mt. Everest or even some of the advanced hiking trails at Yosemite. I've never really been all that close with Sammy Davis Jr. or Burt Reynolds and I'm lousy at frisbee. From reading the above, one might think that I haven't experienced much at all, that I've been locked in a closet all my life. Well, not exactly. I have seen totally insane people and have been within a breath of insanity myself. I have hit the absolute height of joy and depth of depression and have known a wide variety of people, all of which I've made a superhuman effort to understand. Locked in a closet, hardly.

Being a product of a broken home gave me a very dim view of men in general, since my mother spoke all evil and no good about any of the ones she knew, my father especially. If it weren't for my grandfather who sort of filled in the blanks for me, I don't know what would have become of me.

I'll say one thing for myself as a child, I was fat! It's hard enough, just growing up. But growing up with a constant condition of obesity is, I promise you, no fun. Needless to say, I know what it's like to be teased about your figure. As a junior higher, I was too stupid to see through the phoniness of popularity and as a conse-

quence I was constantly trying to fit in with the "in crowd." Because
of this, I was in a cloud of endless anxiety. Now, though, I see some
of the ex-jet setters with a bum for a spouse and a couple of runny-
nosed, ratty-haired dependents. At least my fat saved me from something.

At the high school level, however, I had given up on the idea of
being popular and developed more realistic ideas on a social position
for myself. I settled for real things rather than the tinsel- and glamor-
filled life of a high school cheerleader. I even got some kind of
strange notion that the things I saw around me — student council,
band, homecoming, jocks, cliques, and just high school society in
general — were wazinga, or alternately, bullshit. I hated it all and
found peace only in an art class I took with two really terrific heads,
Maurice and Flash. Those two are folks that I'll never forget. They
were always talking about how many kilos they'd purchased lately,
how full of shit the principal was, and how they'd like to rape the
head cheerleader on the 50-yard line at halftime. I thought them to
be packed full of the reality of it all.

It happened to me in my senior year. What every girl waits for all
of her puberty, her first love. A brilliant University of California-
Davis reject whose worldly possessions were one yellow Volkswagen
beetle (with sunroof), a really fine stereo system, $300 worth of
stereo records, a Wilson tennis racket, three tennis balls that worked
right and 40 that didn't, and a pair of crusty old track shoes. I forgot
one last thing, myself. I'm sure that it was love, pretty sure, anyhow.
One can never tell about something so abstract as love. Besides, I
don't know if a person is capable of love at 17 or 18.

I have just recently found out that my very favorite place in the
whole world was in that Volkswagen on a spring day with the sunroof open and the radio blaring Don McLean's "Vincent" at us as we
looked for a place to "get lost." I can remember the smell of the
thing, even. You know, that sports car smell. And then whenever we
went anyplace classy, he would wear Brut aftershave. It drove me

wild with passion and he knew it. You're probably wondering if this is all a one-sided fantasy on my part and if there ever was a brilliant Davis reject with a yellow Volkswagen. Well, boys and girls, yes there was and it was not just a one-sided fantasy. He admitted to involvement more than I ever did. That surprises me, that I would never admit my feelings for him.

Maybe that was my mistake, my silent tongue. For one rainy April day it all came to an end. We were playing football in the rain with some mutual friends and I knew that something was wrong for sure. Not a smile could be seen on my love's lips. No happiness in his eyes and no affectionate looks for me, either. When he took me home that afternoon, we sat there in silence in my favorite place. I looked around, knowing that this would be my last good look at it, ever. There was the black interior, all textured and leathery. The new VW emblem recently installed on the door of the glove compartment and the new steering wheel cover, all leathery and textured to match the interior. At last, but not at all least, a single strand of hair belonging to your humble narrator that hung continuously from the rear view mirror. There it was, the smell of my favorite place surrounding me and little droplets of rain beading together and running down the dwarfsized windshield and off the ends of my love's hair. I knew what was coming.

He began to speak, but I could have done the talking and said everything he did. This was it. The end. He was going to see the world very soon in my favorite place. He didn't want to hesitate about leaving and so he was going to get the thing that would make him hesitate the most, myself, out of the way. Even before he was through talking the tears were welling up in both of our eyes. However, both of us being strong, dignified Scorpios, neither would try to help the situation by lowering our defenses and admitting our need for the other. So there I sat in misery in my very favorite place in the whole world, taking my last look around.

I cried myself to sleep every night for months afterward, and sometimes I didn't even wait until I was in bed and away from the staring eyes of strangers who couldn't understand. My love for him had been like a candle in the black of night. Delicate, soft, adding life and brightness to an otherwise pointless void. Then, living up to its ephemeral expectations, gone, and without a moment's warning.

Contrary to my wishes, the sun kept coming up and life trudged on. None of it pains me now. It's just a nice remembrance from my past to be treasured for a lifetime. Ah yes, my lifetime. I know not what it holds in store for me. Better times, I hope, for myself and my friends.

$\mathcal{A}$ wen is a benign encysted tumor of the scalp. I have two wens on my scalp. I am trying to decide whether or not to have them removed. The decision medically is an easy one, but based on my experience of having three wens removed before, the decision is made more complicated.

A few years ago, my barber noticed three lumps about one-half inch high and about the size of a quarter on my scalp. He asked me about them and when I told him I had never noticed them before, he suggested I consult a doctor. Quite naturally, I was concerned and saw my doctor soon after leaving the barber shop. My doctor informed me that they were wens, and that he would be able to remove them in the out-patient ward of the hospital. I was quite relieved to learn that it would be a small operation. I made arrangements with him to have them removed the following week.

I reported to the out-patient ward at the hospital at the prescribed time and was told to go to one of the preparation rooms. Soon a nurse came in with a bar of soap, a safety razor, and a bottle of collodion merc. After lathering the bar of soap, she soaked the three areas of my scalp and tried to shave them. Instead of using scissors and cutting the hair short and then shaving, she just tugged and hacked away at my scalp. There was no pain, but I kept wondering whether or not she was going to shave the wen right off, as she tugged and jerked the razor.

Miraculously, she succeeded in shaving the areas without cutting me. I reached into my pocket and got out a quarter and handed it to her, and told her to buy a new blade so the next patient would not have to go through what I did. She assured me that it was a new blade when she started, laughed, and kept my quarter. Next she applied the collodion merc to the hair around the shaved area.

In a few minutes the collodion merc dried hard and held the hair out of the shaved areas. The preparation was over, and now it was the doctor's turn. He soon came in and carefully inspected the shaved areas, and after finding them satisfactory he asked the nurse for a syringe.

Up until the time he called for a syringe, it had not occurred to me how he would administer the anesthetic. I had just assumed it would be sodium pentothal or some other general anesthetic, but now I knew he was going to stick a needle in my head. The thought of it sent shivers up my spine and I broke out in a cold sweat. I must have turned pale, because the doctor grabbed my arm to keep me from falling off the chair. He helped me onto the table and had me lie face down. I mentally fought with myself as to whether it was too late or not to get the hell out of there before he stuck that needle in my head. His firm hand helped settle the question.

I felt the needle penetrate my scalp, and I pushed my head down on the table so hard I thought my nose would split. I don't know how far he injected the needle into my head, but it felt like a mile. I could feel the pressure as the novocaine, or whatever the syringe contained, spread out. The feeling was nauseating and I tried not to think about it. I tried to think of something pleasant. Just about the time I psyched myself into a pleasant situation, the doctor let go of the syringe, with it still stuck in my head. I could feel it twang like an arrow in a target. The doctor explained that it was hard to tell how long it would take to remove the wens, so he would just leave the syringe implanted in my head to facilitate further injections. He made an analogy that he found amusing, something about a double-parked car and the syringe in my head; I failed to see the humor in it.

He proceeded with the operation, and I continued to mash my nose against the table. When it was all over and the arrow was removed from the target, and he had my head full of stitches instead of lumps, he sent for some coffee for me as the nurse wiped the perspiration from my face. After two or three cups of coffee I managed to make it out to my car. The fresh air smelled good as it washed the super-sanitary odor of the hospital from my smashed nose.

It took almost a month to comb the collodion merc out of my hair without pulling the stitches apart. I can remember having a cold after the operation, and every time I sneezed it felt like I was ripping the stitches out.

With all of the memories of that last operation still with me, I'm somewhat reluctant to undergo the same thing again.

*B*eing overweight isn't much fun. I was a chubby little baby and I can't remember being thin. I really started to gain weight when I was about 14 years old and by the time I was a junior in high school I was 40 pounds overweight. My mother took me to one of those pill doctors and I quickly lost all 40 pounds. I had never been so slim in my life, but it didn't last long. Soon after I went off those diet pills I gained back 10 pounds. But that was just the beginning.

Then I was married and I suddenly was out from under mother's thumb and thought I could eat anything I wanted, just like my husband did. Trouble was he never gained a pound. Well, the pounds slowly crept on again. I went to another doctor and he helped me lose a little, but then Dan went into the Army and we moved away. I didn't contact another doctor and I was so bored to tears with being alone in a town where I knew no one that the pounds kept coming back on. I tried to ignore them, but they were there for all the world to see.

Then we moved to Virginia for a while and I was further away from family and friends. I couldn't understand why I was gaining like I was, but I kept putting it from my mind. Then we were sent to Alaska and we were there for three years. Well, there was nothing to do in Alaska but eat, sleep, and make love. I did a lot of all three, but mostly the first.

I did go to a doctor at the Air Force hospital, but the doctor insulted me and wouldn't believe a thing I said, so I left him and stayed away from a doctor for another four years. I was sure I would never get any help from any of them, so I went further into my shell and tried not to think of myself as fat. My husband never said anything to encourage me to lose weight, and I never ended up with any close friends to help me because of the many moves we made. So I was very much alone with my problem.

When we returned home after three years, I was so ashamed I could hardly stand to face my relatives and friends. They didn't say much, but their faces showed how they felt. My mother just said, "You should really go on a diet." Somehow I got through all that and we were swiftly sent off to Italy for another three years.

This time I kept myself so busy with my secretarial job and traveling that I didn't think too much about weight gains, but I knew I was gaining. It was so inexpensive for us to eat out that we did so nearly every night. This didn't help my weight problem, but the food was oh so good. Then one day I hit 200 pounds and I couldn't believe my eyes. I never told Dan, I was too ashamed.

Shortly after that we moved to Washington, D.C., and I became pregnant, after nearly nine years of marriage. The doctor told me he didn't want to see me again if I came in with a weight gain. Well, there was no running this time, so I got to work and started losing weight. I weighed 225 pounds when I first went in to that doctor and after the baby was born I weighed 195 pounds. The doctor was very proud of me.

Then my husband decided to get out of the Army and try television as a career. So we moved back home again. All the pressure of not having an income for three months and having to live with my mother was just too much for me, and I gained back the weight I had lost, plus some. My mother sent me to her doctor, but after two months he told me, "If you don't lose more weight, then I don't want anything to do with you and you might as well leave." That's just what I did. I got up off that table and walked out. That got me so mad at myself that I began to wonder what my problem really was. I knew I could lose weight, I had just done it under the hardest conditions possible, and I was going to do it again.

I had read about Weight Watchers and TOPS, so I started calling around to find out more about them. I decided Weight Watchers was too expensive for me ($3 weekly) and when I got on the phone to the TOPS representative I knew I had suddenly found my place. She wouldn't let me off the phone until I had made a commitment that I would give TOPS a try. I'll never forget that lady — she's remained a close friend these past years.

Attending that first meeting of TOPS (Take Off Pounds Sensibly) was probably the hardest thing I've ever done in my life. Opening the door to find all those women looking at me really made me feel 10 feet wide. I felt like I was the largest one there, but I wasn't. Now I weighed 236 pounds and on my small five-foot, 2½-inch frame that made me look like a very large square. Well, the girls were very friendly and I suddenly found myself talking about my problem and finding out that other people have the same problem too. It was a relief and a big help just to be able to talk about it. It took me six months to be able to say "I'm fat" out loud, and that was a big step in the right direction.

I've gone from a person who stayed in the back of the room and never said a word to eventually become the leader of 60 girls in a new chapter. I've gone down from 236 pounds to 178 pounds and it took me over two years. But I've learned how to control myself and not keep gaining. I can eat only 700 to 800 calories a day to lose weight, and to maintain my weight I stay at about 1200 to 1400 calories, which is what most people diet on. But I'm not alone, there are many other gals in this position.

I've learned that I'm a real slowpoke when it comes to diets. I can stay on one for about three months and lose well, but then I lose interest and get bored and don't lose anything for another three months. That's why it has taken me so long. Most important, I've

104

learned where my problem began, or rather I've learned to face up to it. I had a very lonely and miserable childhood. My mother worked in the day and my father worked at night. I went to a day-care center after school and didn't make friends easily. I used to take money from my mother's purse to buy goodies and I guess these helped me feel more loved. My father and I fought continually and he would never listen to anything I had to say. I know this is where it all began.

I made one mistake while I was leader at TOPS, and that was caring more about the other gals than I cared about myself, so I didn't lose anything for a long time and then suddenly gained back 20 pounds. I couldn't believe that it would ever happen to me, but now I feel it was a good lesson. I just can't let my guard down for one minute.

Now that I'm going to have another baby I had hoped that I could lose like I did before, but this doctor won't let me lose a single pound. In fact, I have to gain two pounds each month. I told him it was the first time in my life that a doctor has told me to gain weight. We both laughed, but it isn't funny and I know it.

I'm determined that when this baby is born I'm going to really get on the ball and lose all of my weight. I have everything going for me now and I want to be slim for myself, my husband, and my children. I don't want them to be ashamed of me, and I don't want them to have any problem either. So far my little girl is slender and eats sensibly — and also gets her sweets so she doesn't have to steal for them.

I'm thankful for TOPS and the way it's helped me to change my life. I've come out of my shell and I'm able to face my problem now and do something about it. Most of all I'm enjoying life more, but I'm looking forward to the time, real soon, when I'll be able to enjoy it to the fullest and no longer have people staring at me because I'm fat or having children laugh at the funny fat lady.

I loathe San Francisco. I lived there for 20 years yet recall few good memories and many bad ones. I enjoyed my nurse's training at Saint Mary's Hospital. I enjoyed my boyfriend, and we spent many happy hours exploring places of interest.

I had spent my childhood in the country. I found the city apartments confining, the cement sidewalks and streets cold and hard, the congestion of people and traffic nerve-wracking. My free time was spent in Golden Gate Park among the trails and tennis courts.

After nurse's training I married the boyfriend and we lived in the box-type, compact home typical of San Francisco, in a nice neighborhood. I was busy with the children, the house, and the small yard. We depended on the city for transportation, friendships, and recreation. We were involved with the schools and the church. We were baseball coaches and Girl Scout leaders. We enjoyed the activity and involvement.

Then the environment slowly changed. Minority groups moved into sections of San Francisco, using the facilities yet adding no improvements. Old neighborhoods deteriorated and old homes became slums. Beatniks and later hippies were seen begging from or harassing people. Tourists flocked to see the Flower Children and in doing so destroyed our Golden Gate Park. The drug pushers moved in and destroyed many individuals. Now robberies and street crimes increased.

106

Our neighbors lived in pressured times and became more short-tempered, less kind, and more intolerant of our children. The children were unsafe in parks unless supervised. They reacted badly to impolite remarks from neighbors. Some neighbors discussed problems well, others became cold and distant, others screamed and yelled, and some called the police. We became defensive and grossly nervous.

One son was nearly molested by a glue-sniffing freak. Another son was chased by a rock-throwing gang. Another son was robbed by a stick-wielding gang on his way to play golf. Our daughter had her pocket picked on a crowded bus. My neighbor suffered permanent brain damage by a purse snatcher who banged her head against a wall. No longer were our children safe. No longer could I walk safely with or without a purse. I no longer attended evening meetings or classes. The last event was when we discovered our oldest son was involved with the growing drug scene. Here our whole purpose in life, our principles and guidelines, were being attacked.

We left San Francisco with no remorse. We are not surrounded by cement, harassed people, congestion, or undesirable elements. The city experience has made our children aware yet not destroyed. San Francisco has many problems, but we won't be there if help is needed. I only wish we had left sooner.

*A*lright, line up for club attacks." The voice isn't that of a drill sergeant, but the result is the same, everyone moves without question of authority. The voice belongs to Professor Charles Gaylord, who holds the rank of seventh degree black belt. He has practiced the style of karate known as kajukembo for 20 years. He is Hawaiian, dark-skinned, dark-haired. He's probably 5-ft. 9-in., but looks shorter because he's so heavily built. To look at him you would think him not very quick, but he's agile as a cat.

The class is lined up in a single-file line in front of a large 8-ft. by 12-ft. mat. The first three in line are black-belt instructors under Gaylord. Everyone else is lined up behind them. The first black-belt student comes up, his name is Norm. The professor tosses him the club and Norm comes at the professor with an overhead attack. The professor steps to the left, blocks Norm's downcoming arm with his right arm, drives his first two knuckles into Norm's ribs, then with the twist of his body strikes Norm's arm behind the elbow and slams Norm, face first, into the mat.

The next club attack is more complicated and much more dangerous. If not enough control is used, you can kill someone. In short, it involves a take-down using the club against your opponent's throat as leverage to throw him. The professor demonstrates the attack with Norm, then throws the club to Jim, the next student. It sails by Jim

111

without being caught; he isn't paying attention. The professor's eyes open wide.

Everyone in the class knows what is coming next, especially Jim. Jim takes the club and tries an overhead attack on the professor. The professor seems at first to repeat the first attack by moving to the left and blocking Jim's arm. But the professor circles his arm clockwise 270 degrees so that instead of Jim's arm being up above the professor's forehead it is now down to the left of the professor's body. He kicks Jim in the groin, reaches under Jim's outstretched arm with his free hand and takes the club. Then he simply rotates his wrist so that half the club rests across Jim's throat. The professor stops a moment almost as if to let the suspense sink in.

Then before we can blink our eyes Jim's head snaps back as his feet leave the mat and he lands with a thud. Before anyone really grasps how that must have felt, the professor kicks Jim in the side of the face with the ball of his foot. He slaps Jim's body a few more times for good measure before finishing. He has gotten his point across very well.

Jim gets up, his eyes glassy, his face red, either from embarrassment or the slap of the foot across the cheek. I can see Jim running his tongue inside his mouth to keep his lower lip from quivering. He is a young man and crying would be worse than the punishment he just went through. The male pride is really something else.

The professor turns and tosses me the club. I grab on to it like my life depends on it. I'm not going to make a mistake.

Later on Norm goes up to Jim and asks, "Are you going to take that from Gaylord?" Jim smiles and says, "You're damn right." They both laugh and class resumes.

*A*ll week I had eagerly anticipated our family outing to San Francisco. We were going first to the Recreational Vehicle Show at the Cow Palace, and then to the beach for a picnic lunch and fun in the surf. Sunday morning arrived and I dressed, prepared breakfast, and supervised the children's dressing and grooming. After packing the lunch, I went outside to report to my husband that we were ready to go. He was tinkering on his truck and said that he would finish in a minute and get cleaned up so we could go. I went back inside and busied myself with housework.

An hour later I went outside to find my husband still puttering, without showing the least indication of getting ready to go on the excursion we had planned for the day. I became impatient and made the statement that I was fed up with him saying one thing and doing another. I then returned to the house to be followed shortly by the man I had been married to for nine years. He had been angered by my statement and a brief argument ensued. When I saw that his anger was building, I became quiet except for an occasional comment in my defense. As I stood by helplessly, he worked himself into a rage. Caustic words grew into shouts and profanity. Like a shark at the smell of blood, he by the sound of his yelling excited his anger to the point of irrationality. Realizing my danger, I stopped being openly defensive and attempted a tack of agreement and reassurance. But he was past the point of no return. The floodgates were open and the hostility poured forth upon me through the vehicles of his closed fists and strong arms. I was struck in the face, on my head, and on my shoulders. I tried to protect my head with my hands and arms.

As he hit me over and over again, I knew that he wanted to kill me. I found myself on the floor and saw that he was kicking me, but I didn't feel it. I was pleading with him and promised always to do whatever he wished. He paused long enough for me to stand up, but he was again gripped by violent impulses. With his hands squeezing my throat, he threatened, "I'm going to strangle you until your eyes bulge." I pulled at his hands but found it impossible to pry them off. For an instant the thought of dying entered my head, but I would not accept that fate. I closed my eyes to pray and think of a method of escape, when suddenly he threw me down and left the house. Throughout the whole incident, I was numb. My mind worked in ways unfamiliar. I wasn't consciously thinking, but thoughts did occur to me and I acted upon them immediately as best I could. My defense was verbal: I knew instinctively that for me to hit or kick at him would serve only to increase his fury.

I looked in the mirror and saw that my face was already swollen in several places, and a purple coloration was evident below one eye. There was only one laceration, and it was bleeding slightly. My throat was bruised. I put on my sun glasses, gathered my three sons together, and we got into the car and drove off. We didn't come back that day.

This wasn't the first time my husband had succumbed to a fit of rage. There had been broken dishes, windows, and appliances, and holes in the wall. On one other occasion, he had beaten me so that I required emergency medical attention. My nose was cauterized and packed to stop the bleeding.

I'm going to have to change my life. I can not—and will not—subject myself to further abuse.

*T*oday I was exposed to the evils of gambling! Michael and I had gone into Berkeley with the intention of purchasing two tickets to a Joan Baez concert. Then we were going to leave Berkeley as fast as we had come, go back to Pleasant Hill and finish our homework. However, we ended up spending more time and money than we had intended.

We drove into Berkeley at about 4 p.m., parked the truck and walked up a few streets till we hit Bancroft Avenue, then walked down Bancroft until we came to the student union. There we bought the Joan Baez tickets at the ASUC box office and then walked outside and sat down on the steps of the student union to watch the Hare Krishna chanters.

We sat on the steps for quite a while asking each other questions about the Hare Krishna religion, which neither one of us could answer. Finally one of the chanters came up and started telling us about the Hare Krishna chant. He was dressed in orange material draped around his body with a tee shirt underneath, and rubber thongs on his feet. His voice was very raspy which I suppose was due to all the chanting. His face and head were shaved clean except for a spot of hair growing on the back of his head.

He told us about how the chanting brought a person closer to God and how man must learn to give up material values, which can never give him any satisfaction.

Michael asked him a lot of questions while I half listened and half thought to myself about all of the different religions and meditation groups and yoga groups. How each one claims to know the way to God and a better level of consciousness.

The Hare Krishna fellow left—his last words to us were "Hare Krishna" (which means "praise God")—and Mike and I got up to walk back to the car. We decided to go back by way of Telegraph Avenue. We were still talking about Hare Krishna and their ideas of giving up all material things, when we came upon a group of people on the sidewalk, all clustered around one fellow who was doing something with cards. Mike was more interested than I in sticking around to watch the people gamble their money, on a guess as to which card was the right one to get twice your money. The game that was being played with the cards was similar to the old pea and shell game where a person mixes up three shells, one of them with a pea under it. While shuffling the shells around, the person shuffling occasionally lifts various shells which give the person watching an idea as to which shell has the pea beneath it. Applying this idea to cards, the shuffler uses two black cards and one red card. The object being to decide where the red card is, and sometimes the shuffler even shows all three as he places them down at the end of his shuffling.

As I said before, Michael seemed to be more interested in watching this, and I had a hard time seeing over the heads of the people gathered around the shuffler, so I went into a nearby dime store and returned to the huddle of people. Mike told me that a person had just lost $60 by betting $20 three times and losing every bet. I just shook my head and I heard Mike saying, "Don't you feel the urge to gamble?" I thought to myself that, no, I didn't feel any urge to gamble and lose my money.

A girl sitting below us had been betting and winning until she finally won all of the money that the shuffler had. That ended the game and everyone split up. A guy that had been standing next to us said that the game had been fixed, and that the girl who had just won all of the shuffler's money probably worked with him.

Mike and I started walking down the street again and stopped in a few shops. We crossed a street and found another group of people huddled around another shuffler, or should I call him a hustler? This guy was showing the cards as he put each down on its face so that it was almost impossible to miss. He would lay the cards down, look up and stare at all the faces around him and say, "Who saw that, who's willing to lay 10 or 20 down and pick up that red card?" Then if no one said anything he'd go around the circle and ask certain people.

I had seen it, so when he came around to me and said, "Did you see it?" I said, "Yes." After telling him that I'd seen it he replied, "Well, give me $10 and I'll give you $20." I shook my head and mumbled that I didn't have $10 but I'd do it for one dollar. One dollar seemed like a lot of money to me, and besides that I didn't have more than a dollar bill in my pocket. But as I said, one dollar seemed like a lot to me and I did feel the urge to gamble, as Mike had put it earlier.

Now I was out of the game as far as the shuffler was concerned because he wanted at least $10. Somehow a guy behind us started talking to us and all three of us would watch and agree on what we thought we had seen. Suddenly this third guy put up $10 and turned over a black card. He left about as quickly as he had come, while Mike and I continued to watch the game. Then it was Mike's turn; he offered $10 and the shuffler kept trying to make him go to 20 but Mike stayed at 10. The shuffler took the bill and Mike looked at me and said, "The one in the middle?" I nodded. He bent over and turned the card up. It was black.

Hare Krishna!

I remember the day you stood before us and handed out essays other students had written. You told us that this represented some of the work that had been turned in before, and that the papers were examples of types of experiences we could write about. One particular paper was written about a girl and her boyfriend who lost $10 gambling in Berkeley. I was amused at the thought of someone wasting his money at a game of chance. Otherwise, the essay did not make too much of an impression on me and I soon forgot it. However, on July 4th that particular essay jolted back into my memory.

I was home alone since my folks were spending the three-day weekend at Lake Tahoe. My cousin had called earlier that morning and asked if I would go to the county fair with him and his family. I had nothing planned, so I accepted his invitation. I was to meet them at their home at noon. As soon as I arrived, everything was put in their car and we were off for the fair. Once there, my cousin and I went one way and my aunt and uncle another. We agreed to meet at the garden show at 4 p.m.

Many more people were at the fair than I had anticipated. I remember thinking that a person could feel very lonely here even among 90,000 people. People were very cold toward us, and I suppose we must have seemed very cold toward them. A fair or other large gathering destroys the friendship between people. It seems you are out for yourself and everyone else is shut out.

We walked about the fair for nearly an hour, spending small amounts of money at booths and snack huts. We finally found ourselves at one end of the fair with a small number of people and a lot of booths. As we were looking at the booths, one man leaned forward from behind a counter and asked us to come over. We looked at each other, then walked over to see what he had to say.

The man was tall and appeared to be around 40. His face looked tired and drawn. Scars marked his forehead and cheeks, giving me the impression that this fellow had been in his share of scrapes. He wore very conservative clothing and spoke in a sly, demanding whisper.

He looked down at us and told us since business was slow, he'd give us a special deal. He set up before us a small wooden block and gave us three chances to ring the block and win a large stuffed dog. The blocks were rectangular with a slight uphill grade. All we had to do to win was to toss a ring over the block. Originally, it took all three rings to win the dog, but in our case all we needed to do was to ring one.

I gave him a dollar and as quickly as he took it I had lost it. He looked at me and said he'd move the block closer because he really wanted me to win. Out came another dollar, and into his pocket it went. Normally, I'm a tight person but I swear that man must have cast a spell over me. He moved the block closer yet, and another dollar was disposed of. Finally, the block was directly in front of me, and I still could not put the ring over it. I was down to my last dollar when I had to use all my strength to break away from him. He turned away in disgust and I left in a daze. I soon realized what had happened to me and I was filled with rage. This indeed was a lesson well learned.

Hare Krishna!

I went to a wedding reception a few nights ago and observed some conventional, very sociable behavior patterns on the part of the participants. These observations were made under the influence of champagne, and it was not until the following day that I realized it was possible material to write about. So I may not report the things that happened in their proper sequence, but it was their nature that mattered.

Let me try and set the scene first. John and Diane, the persons getting married, are both young and beautiful. I am acquainted only with the groom, and it is his behavior that I wish to reflect upon. He acted in accordance with some cultural habits that I personally would like to see die out. But it seems as though it may take awhile. Change comes slowly.

When I got to the reception hall, it came to my attention that I was the only one dressed casually. So, casually, I took a seat with some other guests in chairs lined up against one of the walls. John, the groom, was making some sort of a thank-you speech into a microphone in front of all the tables and chairs, right next to the champagne fountain. Relieved, I saw two other friends across the room.

They were Sue and Hank, engaged to be married. I walked over to them, and we all three sipped champagne, chatted, and observed the family members of the newlyweds do comical and drunken things.

John's parents were lighting up the dance floor with their own version of the twist.

John and Hank at one time were heavy rivals in the pursuit of the affections of Sue. Sue is a very beautiful, sincere person. I've always liked her. And since her recent engagement to Hank, I've never seen her happier.

John was just beaming throughout the entire evening. He and his new bride were busily talking to everyone present, and they were visibly enjoying themselves. At one point, John dismissed himself from a conversation with his brother, who was also best man, and came over to ask Sue for a dance. This is when I caught the gist of a weird situation that is connected with weddings and is part of my reasons for suspicion of the whole process.

John did not speak directly to Sue, but asked Hank for permission to dance with her. Hank obliged and then there was a series of remarks made by John, the essence of which was: "You don't have to worry now, Hank, I'm officially tied to another woman. I wouldn't get caught doing anything to jeopardize Sue's relationship with you, even though I might still like to. Ha! Ha! I'll even give you permission to dance with my wife, sort of as compensation for stepping on an old rival's toes." I thought for a moment I was at an auction. Sue, the merchandise sitting next to me, was blushing pink.

After all this rhetoric, the couple finally went to the dance floor. Then I saw John say a few words directly to Sue. I was left sitting there with Hank. He was fidgeting and watching Sue more frequently than not. Before the music ended, he got up and cut in, sweeping Sue away after leaving me with the protest, "I better do something before she gets paranoid."

These two young competitors, John and Hank, are my peers. It rather shocked me to hear them speaking to each other like middle-aged men. It saddens me to think that they value human life so little. If they feel they must push and compete in the realm of such a basic human relationship as one between a man and a woman, then I think they shall probably both over-exert their energies at an early age.

In 20 years John and Hank may meet again at a cocktail party or another wedding and still be rivals, not truly friends. Only this time, their source of competition will undoubtedly involve money. It will be a bragging session about how much stock one or the other of them owns, or how many cars each of them has. They might some day get to be good friends, but not as long as their relationship is dominated by this competitive drive instilled so deep in each of them. But such is the fabric of our American way of life, and I suppose somebody has to carry it on.

*I*t all started when my sister sent us an original Christmas gift from Hawaii—all the trimmings for a luau. Snow was falling in our Virginia suburb of Washington, D.C., so we put up the package to save it for warmer weather.

The gift was prophetic. With an early spring came word that neighbors had been transferred to Honolulu. We dusted off the Christmas box; it would make a fine start on a going-away party.

My husband, Ron, loves parties. He tends to get enthusiastic when plans are being made. You could even say that, together, we are apt to be carried away by good intentions.

"What we need is a pig," I said, getting into the spirit.

Ron agreed, "Why don't you scout around and try to get a suckling pig and we'll have a real luau."

"A pig . . . yeah." A hint of sanity crept into my voice.

"Well, here we are in the heart of hog growing country; someone must have one to sell." My husband has great faith in my ingenuity.

The next morning I rang the buzzer over the meat counter at the A&P. "Where do you keep your pigs?" I asked. It seemed the best plan, just brazen it out.

"What?" the butcher shouted quite rudely.

"Pigs. You know, like in French recipes . . . and luaus." I answered as though I bought a pig there every week.

"Lady, we ain't got no pigs." He closed the glass partition that

125

protected him from unreasonable housewives and refused to answer my further rings.

"French recipes," I mused on my way home. "That's it," I said aloud. There was a small French gourmet food store in Washington that catered to the embassies and I could try there. When I phoned, the man on the other end of the call spoke no English and I no French.

"Pig," I said calmly for the fifth or sixth time. "A small pig . . . oink, oink?"

Something must have clicked in his memory. "Ah, oui, oui . . . tomorrow."

I felt that I had won a major battle until I remembered that it would be my husband's day to drive in the car pool. I phoned back. The language barrier did not come down. Pig and tomorrow were irrevocably linked.

With the luau only three days off, I decided to go along with "tomorrow's pig." Accordingly, I hired a baby sitter for the better part of the day and set off by bus. As always, the monuments on the bridge approaching the Lincoln Memorial caused me to gasp, a pride in my country rising within me. "You can even buy a pig in the capital," I thought smugly.

As I stood awed by the shelves of strange and exotic foods, an elderly man came up and spoke to me in rapid French. I shook my head sadly and asked, "pig?"

"Ah . . . oui." He beamed, bowing slightly, then turned and disappeared through a small door. Soon he returned, carrying a pale gray object over two feet long (and frozen) which he handed to me. It was not very heavy but it was cold. I shuffled it from arm to arm while he told me, in perfect English, the price of my folly.

I paid, asking for a bag. He shrugged; the language barrier again. I made wrapping motions with my hands around the animal now lying on the counter gazing at me.

Success. A quick rustling of paper and my parcel was wrapped;

except that the snout poked out one end of the package. I wished that I had brought a baby blanket; I might have been able to smuggle my purchase aboard the bus under the guise of an incredibly ugly child.

I could not back down after getting this far. Pig and I boarded the homeward-bound bus. I tried to look nonchalant; after all, everyone carries a frozen pig around with them now and then. The pig looked, and felt, cold.

At home, he resided on the kitchen counter, slowly thawing, while I prepared dinner around him.

My husband said he was proud of me; well, partly anyway. "Did you have to buy such a big one?" he asked. I threatened to hit him with a frying pan or go home to Mother, a continent away.

"What's wrong with my pig? I think he's a beauty — among pigs, that is."

"Yes, he's lovely, only where are you going to cook him? He won't fit into the oven." In practical matters, Ron was right, as usual.

The pig did, however, fit on the hand-turned spit my husband and his friend built the next day. The powers to reckon with in our apartment complex were finally persuaded to give us permission to build a temporary fire pit on a little-used walkway behind our apartment.

Our pig was indeed a thing of beauty and the hit of the luau as he rested on our improvised low table with an orange in his mouth. One of my daughters had eaten his apple.

*M*y oldest dog, Princess, had been slipping while walking in the house. I thought it was because she was getting older and losing her balance. My sister told me a few months ago it might be that her toenails were too long. This dog has long matted hair around her feet. I have her trimmed like a poodle once a year and her year is well over.

I said I would check her nails first chance I got. I forgot about it until yesterday when she nearly fell three times in a few feet. Her nails were two inches long and curling under. No wonder she couldn't walk. She has spent this whole year growing nails. I grabbed her and hollered for Larry, my oldest son, to get the nail clippers. The dog always knows when I am going to do something to her and takes off for under the bed.

I cut her front nails and she yelped with every other nail. The vet told me it doesn't hurt to cut the nails, unless you get too high on the nail and cut a blood vessel. So I kept telling her, "It doesn't hurt, shut up."

While she and I were discussing toenails, Snapper, the younger dog, was staring at Princess. She dislikes Princess. Every time Princess yelped, Snapper lunged at her. Larry finally had to take Snapper away.

Princess was done. I decided while I had the clippers out I would do Snapper. I knew her dewclaws were curling under and she hasn't had a toenail clipping since she was born.

Snapper has sensitive feet. I don't know why but she feels those feet are sacred, and she proves it by snapping if you even touch her toes. But after all, I am the human here. I weigh over 100 pounds more than she does. So I tucked her under my arm and started in. Such screaming, more than yelping, more than squealing. I only did two toes when I sent Larry for a leash. I was going to make a muzzle.

Walter, my youngest, chose that time to come in and demand, "What are you doing to the dog?"

Larry said, "Get out of here," and gave him a shove.

So I had an angry dog in my lap and a fight in the hall. I used the only weapon available, my voice.

"Walter and Larry, get away from each other!" Big help. Walter finally gave Larry a push and he hit the wall. The phone rang. Walter answered it. It got him away from Larry. It was for me. I took the phone in my right hand and the dog, who had calmed down a little, in my left. It was a telephone saleswoman.

"Mrs. Haas, I rep —" Walter walked past Larry to get back outside. Larry slugged him, as well as a neighbor kid. Now I had three kids screaming and hitting each other. So I calmed them all down again with my weapon.

I screamed at them, "Get outside. Now!"

I talked to the phone in my hand. "I think you can tell you called at the wrong time." She could tell.

Now it was just Snapper, Larry, and I. I made the muzzle. No problem. Snapper was accepting. I told Larry to hold her face. I took her foot in my hand. She started to squirm. I clipped the toenail. Snapper tore loose from the muzzle and bit Larry. Blood squirted from the nail; I had hit a blood vessel.

"Get a wet rag." My solution to everything. I had used the same wet rag earlier on Walter's eye.

The dog was hysterical. The smell of fear was almost overpowering. So we sat with her, held her foot in the wet rag, calmed her down, and finally gave her a whole cookie. She didn't associate with us for the rest of the day. Just lay under a chair and licked her foot and looked pitiful.

She still needs her toenails cut, but I am going to take her to the vet and pay the $7 for the call. He is going to earn it.

I was "behind schedule," caught up in a last-minute conversation, now caught up in traffic. Obviously, they too were late. I made my off-ramp, and two blocks later turned onto the street on which I live. They, naturally, were way ahead of me.

My house, situated on a corner, is really the bottom third of a triplex. I park my car and motorcycle in a carport at the back. Every day, except weekends, I drive past my front door, execute an injudicious right turn at the corner, and then a second one as I enter my driveway. All this, of course, must have been known to them.

On this day, I drove past my front door as usual, taking small notice of a white van parked on the wide gravel shoulder across the street, the traditional parking place for visitors. No one I knew, I was sure. I imagined a pause at the corner, exhibited my usual antics, and raced headlong into the carport. Instantly, I observed . . . THEM. Of course, they also took prompt notice of . . . ME. This confrontation was, necessarily, short-lived. They, a tall, ascetic, pimply-faced beanpole with shoulder-length black hair, and his companion, a shorter but powerfully built brigand with a handlebar moustache, made a hasty exit along the path to the front yard. I fairly leaped from the car and dashed, albeit somewhat cautiously, around the corner in time to catch a glimpse of the pair tumbling into the back of the innocuous van, which immediately roared onto the road, tires smoking.

I stood transfixed, smelling the acrid smoke, watching with fascination the thick oily cloud that marked the passage of the van. Momentarily, I was rushing for the phone.

Like any good, media-fed moron, I knew exactly what to do: call the police, give them all the details, touch nothing 'til the detectives arrive. I dialed the operator and said, "Operator, this is an emergency, get me the police!" Man, what a thrill! I'd always wanted to do that, and now, there it was, perfect, straight out of *Dragnet*. As the operator made the connection, I planned my next lines: "I'd like to report an attempted grand theft, auto. The attempt occurred at 5:12 p.m. The suspects were last seen heading north on Parkside Drive in a late model white Ford van, licen—"

"Walnut Creek police department, may I help you?"

"Somebody tried to steal my bike!" I blurted.

"What?"

"Uh, I'd like to report an attempted theft."

"Could I have your name and address, please?"

I gave it.

"And what was the nature of the attempted theft?"

"They, somebody tried to steal my motorcycle."

"Alright, sir, we'll have an officer there shortly."

"Fine, but look, they just drove off not five minutes ago in a white Ford van—"

"Yes, sir, you can give all that information to the officer. He'll take your complete statement."

"But they're getting away! You could send out a—"

"I understand, sir. Just give that information to the officer. Is there anything else?"

"No."

Click.

I was crushed, this wasn't the way it was supposed to happen. The phone found its way back to the cradle.

I wandered, somewhat dazed, to the carport. Picking my way carefully, so as not to efface any clue, I inspected my bike. Everything looked intact, still chained stoutly to the pole which supports one corner of the carport. Plenty of fingerprints here, no doubt. Wandering, my eyes found a footprint in the recently turned earth at the side of the path, and following this another where a foot had missed the concrete path in hurried retreat. Visions of plaster casts, here was a clue for sure! I began to feel like Holmes on the trail.

None too soon the police arrived. The lone uniformed officer stepped deliberately from his vehicle. He strode determinedly across the yard, carrying the ultimate symbol of his authority: a black leather notebook. After identifying myself, I recounted the incident, somewhat confusedly, and pointed out the many obvious clues, adding that I had been careful to disturb nothing. To this he replied, "Could I see your license and registration, please?" Needless to say, I was taken somewhat aback, but quickly reconciled myself to this prosaic and ponderous system of law enforcement. He then requested the ownership certificate, which I fetched from the house. Returning, I found him leaning over the motorcycle, a hand resting thoughtlessly against the gas tank. Horrified, I asked, as tactfully as possible, if he expected to find many fingerprints? He looked up suddenly, a broad grin spreading across his features. Looking away just as quickly, he commented to the bike, "I don't think we'll be taking any fingerprints at this time." I didn't ask about plaster footprints.

Straightening up, he inquired about a few pertinent details. Dutifully jotting my answers, he remarked casually, "That's a pretty sturdy security chain you have there."

"It ought to be," I answered. "I paid enough for it."

"Case hardened, isn't it?"

"Sure is, so's the lock. No damned bolt cutters ever get through that."

The notebook snapped shut without comment.

With that portentous sound, it struck me that the official investigation of the most heinous and ignoble crime in the history of Christendom was drawing hastily to a close.

"Uh, are you through?" I asked, obviously dismayed.

"I'm going to take a look across the street; and then I'll have you sign a brief, unsworn statement. You'll be notified in a few days as to the disposition of the case."

"Great," I muttered, as the blue uniform crossed to where the white van had stood. He soon returned, looking as if he had just inherited a fortune by way of the demise of a distant uncle. Seldom has anyone tried so hard not to smile. His right hand carried a squat gray cylinder. It seemed about a foot long and maybe half that in diameter, rounded on the bottom, with a narrow neck topped by a small brass valve. Without a word, and to his credit, without a smile, he withdrew from his car a large plastic bag, and deftly dropped the metallic bottle into this repository. Vindication! Surely now good would triumph, and the forces of darkness and evil would be vanquished! But how? What the hell was this piece of super evidence, anyway?

As if to answer, he held the bag at eye level and said with undisguised pride that, as far as he knew, this was the first gas cylinder recovered in connection with a motorcycle theft in the county. "Of course we've been told they're used quite often in the city, and we've recovered some smaller cylinders in connection with bicycle thefts out here, but I'm pretty sure this is the first ti—"

I interrupted to confess my continued ignorance as to the insidious nature and use of these "gas cylinders." This seemed to break his reverie and he explained, in best training manual fashion, that the cylinder contained ordinary carbon dioxide gas, under extreme pressure. The gas, actually a liquid at that pressure, is squirted onto a case-hardened chain, where the instantaneous evaporation rapidly super-cools the steel making it extremely brittle and easy prey for a pair of ordinary bolt cutters.

Leapin' lizards! Shades of James Bond! Cryogenics, the science of super-cold, right there in my own back yard! Batman and Robin versus Captain Icicle, Superman battles the Frost Wizard. The dawn of a new age of crime. The furthest future becomes reality. My mind boggles. I explained all this to the blue uniform. I told him of the prophecy to which his children were privy, and of the tremendous importance of the application of space age technology to crime! He asked me to sign my statement. I tried to explain the great philosophical significance of the crime, how the true measure of the technological level of society was the technical sophistication of the average working man. "These were no mean outlaws," I expounded, "but technological pioneers, bringing the esoteric fruits of space research home to the common man!" The red light faded in the distance.

In retrospect, my actions must have seemed a bit strange to the police. And I must confess, at this point, I'm much more intrigued than distressed by my near disaster. Having recounted the episode to several friends, and all having shown a similar disinclination toward any dissertation on the relationship between Captain America, The Space Program, and The Working Class, it seems only logical that I should let the entire matter drop. But, in fact, I cannot simply forget it. It's all too clear, too painfully obvious. The future unfolds before us. *Scientific American* is out of touch, *Marvel Comix* points the way. Cryogenics, get it? Super-cold super-crime. State-of-the-art, avant-garde, fantastic. Get it? That stuff is old hat to the Fantastic Four. Why, only this morning I was reading about this portable, solid-state, dual-reflecting, ion-focused, solar-powered, gas laser . . .

*I*t was not just another hot Alabama day, but a very special one. Seven days, just one more week, and it would finally be over. Joe Pribela, private citizen. How great that sounded.

As I was driving home from the base, I started reflecting on my life. I was one lucky guy. I had a nice wife and soon there would be a child. To top it all off, the job I had enjoyed so much in the service was being changed to a civilian position. It was to be mine upon release from the service, and instead of the pittance we'd been living on, there would be a sizable increase in income.

As my thoughts turned to my prospective salary, I began to think of a lot of things we needed and would soon be able to afford. My day-dreaming was suddenly interrupted by a really incredible sight.

I had never been a car nut; in fact, here I was at the age of 24 and still driving the first car I ever owned. The incredible sight to which I was referring was a 1964 Buick Riviera. There it sat in the show-room window, and it was a case of love at first sight. I could hardly wait to get a closer look. When I had inspected the car thoroughly, I was a lost man.

I couldn't wait to run home, pick up my wife, and bring her back to see the car. To my consternation, my wife had something to tell me—she was in labor! She quickly assured me that since it was a first baby, it would take a while before it was born. So she felt she might as well make the waiting go faster by looking at my recent discovery.

She loved it as much as I did, and we decided that the only course open was to test drive it, and then discuss costs with the salesman. As we were driving around, my wife was keeping track of how often the contractions were coming. By the time we had climbed out of the car and had been ushered into the salesman's office, the pains were coming eight minutes apart.

As the salesman was talking cost and interest figures to me, I was keeping a running tally of contractions. Every time my wife had a contraction she would give me a nudge, and I would write the time down. The salesman thought he had a hot one here, since he thought I was writing figures on the auto.

After glancing at my sheet, however, he asked what I was doing. Once I explained, his smiling face turned to a frown, and a nervous look appeared on his face. He had visions of delivering a baby in his office. When I mentioned that the pains were five minutes apart, he thought it best to get my wife to the hospital, and to discuss the Riviera at another time. He still remains the only salesman I ever met who was glad to see a prospective customer leave.

No, I never did buy that beautiful, shiny, new Buick Riviera. In the early hours of the morning, I saw my son for the first time, and one look made me think of all the things he'd be needing for his future, and a Buick Riviera didn't quite fill that need. Although that car was still beautiful, it was not anywhere near as beautiful as the 6-pound 13-ounce little boy.

*S*ome things are just unreal, y'know?

The sound of an Old Heap's engine knocking, black fumes pouring out a corroded tail pipe, and the racket of a back seat full of kids.

This mess pulls into Central Drive-in Dairy and Milk Depot, my own salt mine.

"Yes ma'am, may I help you?"

"Ngmph."

"Pardon me, ma'am?"

She turns to smack a kid in the back seat with the flat of a fleshy hand. Bawling ensues, hardly noticeable over the din of the four-wheeled catastrophe.

"Gimme milk."

Her eyes are not on me, or her car, or the dairy, or the scenery. Her eyes are on nothing.

"Yes ma'am. And that will be one half gallon?"

She does something like a nod. I think it's a nod. Her chins ripple.

It must have been a hiccough, because when I return with one half gallon, she scowls at the empty air and says "four."

Not angrily, mind you, because I don't really think she's capable of that sort of thing.

"I'm sorry, ma'am." Not really.

So I bring back four half gallons of homogenized milk.

"I want low-fat," she mumbles, which is really a baritone shriek.

Back I go. Within seconds I return with four half gallons of low-fat milk. Unfortunately, I have not been trained in Second Sight, and I bring back four half gallons of low-fat milk—in cartons.

"Want bottles."

"Yes, ma'am."

In my mind's eye I see my hands encircle her neck. Nope. Too wide.

I'm back with four bottles of low-fat milk and begin to place them ever so gently in a large brown paper sack that nine times out of ten will rip before I get it to the car.

"Will that be all today, ma'am?" I ask so cheerfully that I successfully mask the sound of gritting teeth.

Her chins ripple again, but I'm smart to that now. So without ringing up the sale on our 1918 cash register that works only when you speak nicely to it—in Swedish—I begin to put the bottles in the back seat of the Old Heap (the car, that is).

Well, the door's locked and none of the screaming Back Seat Mob much gives a damn, so I reach through the open front window to pull the lock, and find out that she's brought a very excitable French poodle.

"Down Samson!" she commands in her first display of real life, and I check my hand over to see how badly I've been mauled.

Samson, her seven-pound man eater, is making like he's ready to gore me, snarling and yipping and pawing the windows.

Now about this time she looks at the bag I'm holding, and the one gear in her head slowly turns to register the fact that "You don't have my rack."

A rack, by the way, is a metal carrier that holds four milk bottles, and it seems that she's brought one, bottles and all, to be refilled. And it's sitting somewhere amidst the Back Seat Mob being guarded by a seven-pound ferocious lump of curls named Samson.

Now it's no story when I tell you that fiascos like this represent almost 85% of my working hours.

Some things are just unreal, y'know?

NO PICNICING
OR LOITERING ...
ALLOWED IN THIS PARK

PHOTOGRAPH CREDITS